This book belongs to :

____

Table of contents :

Joint The Dots To Trace The Lines.

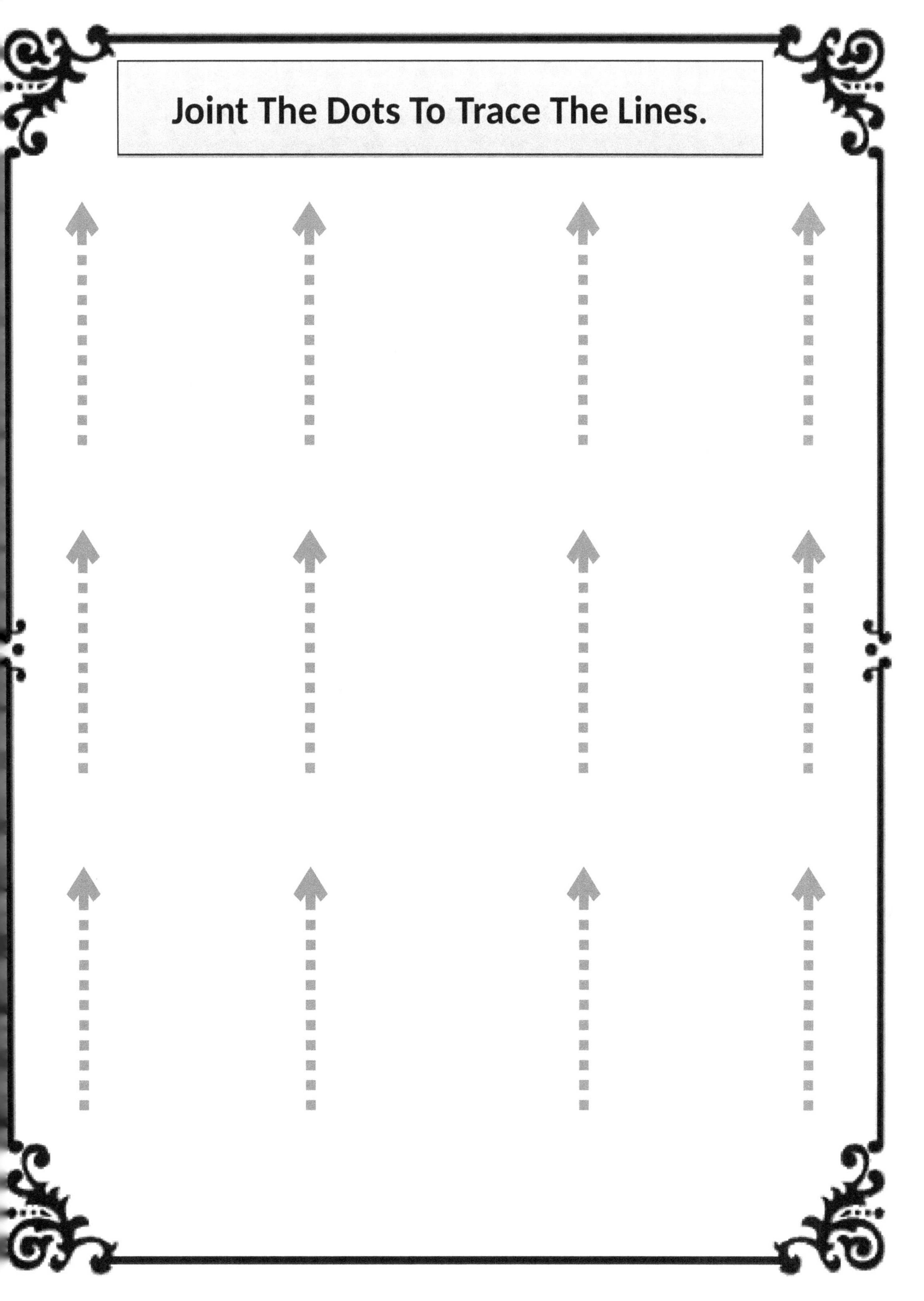

Joint The Dots To Trace The Lines.

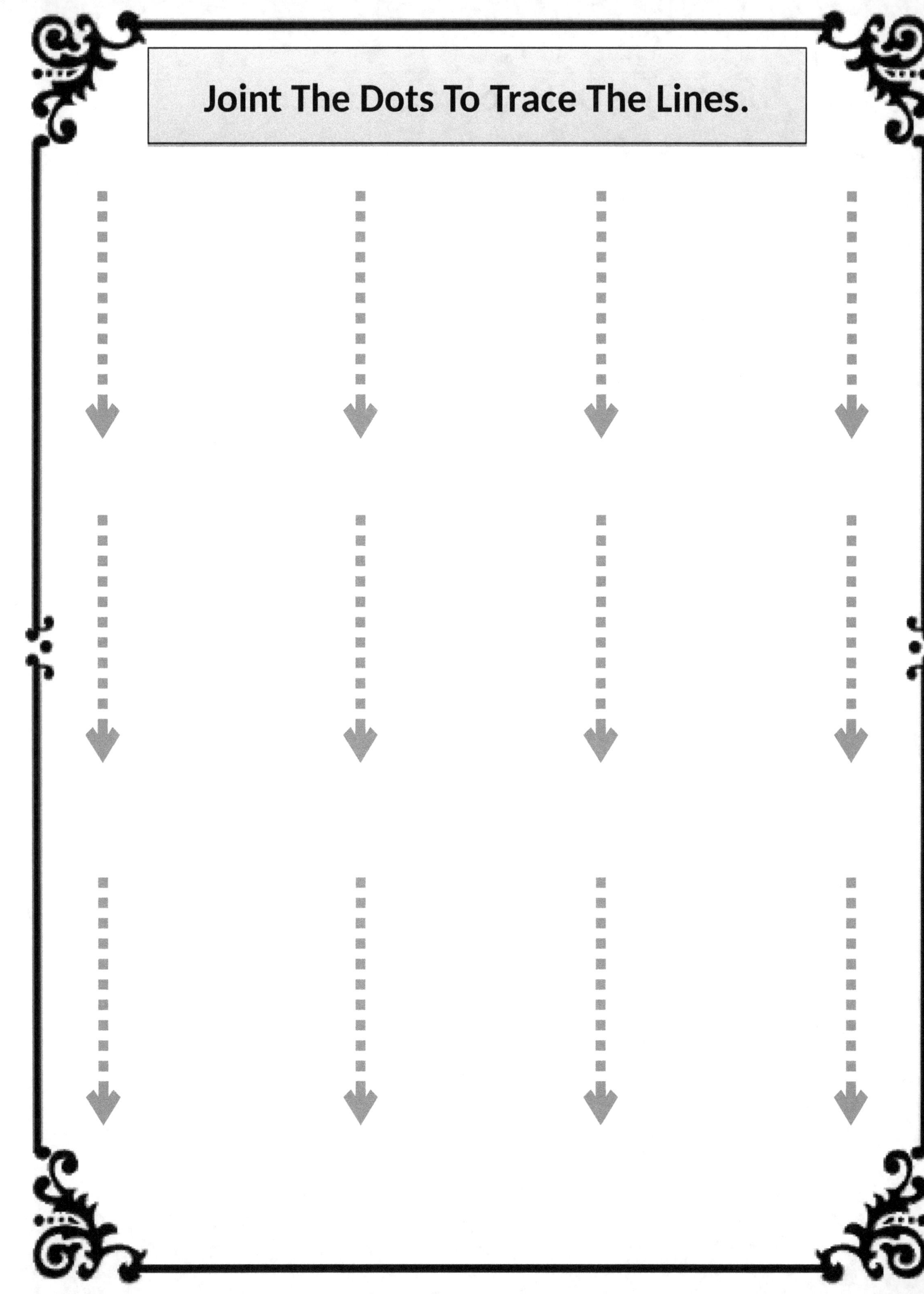

Joint The Dots To Trace The Lines.

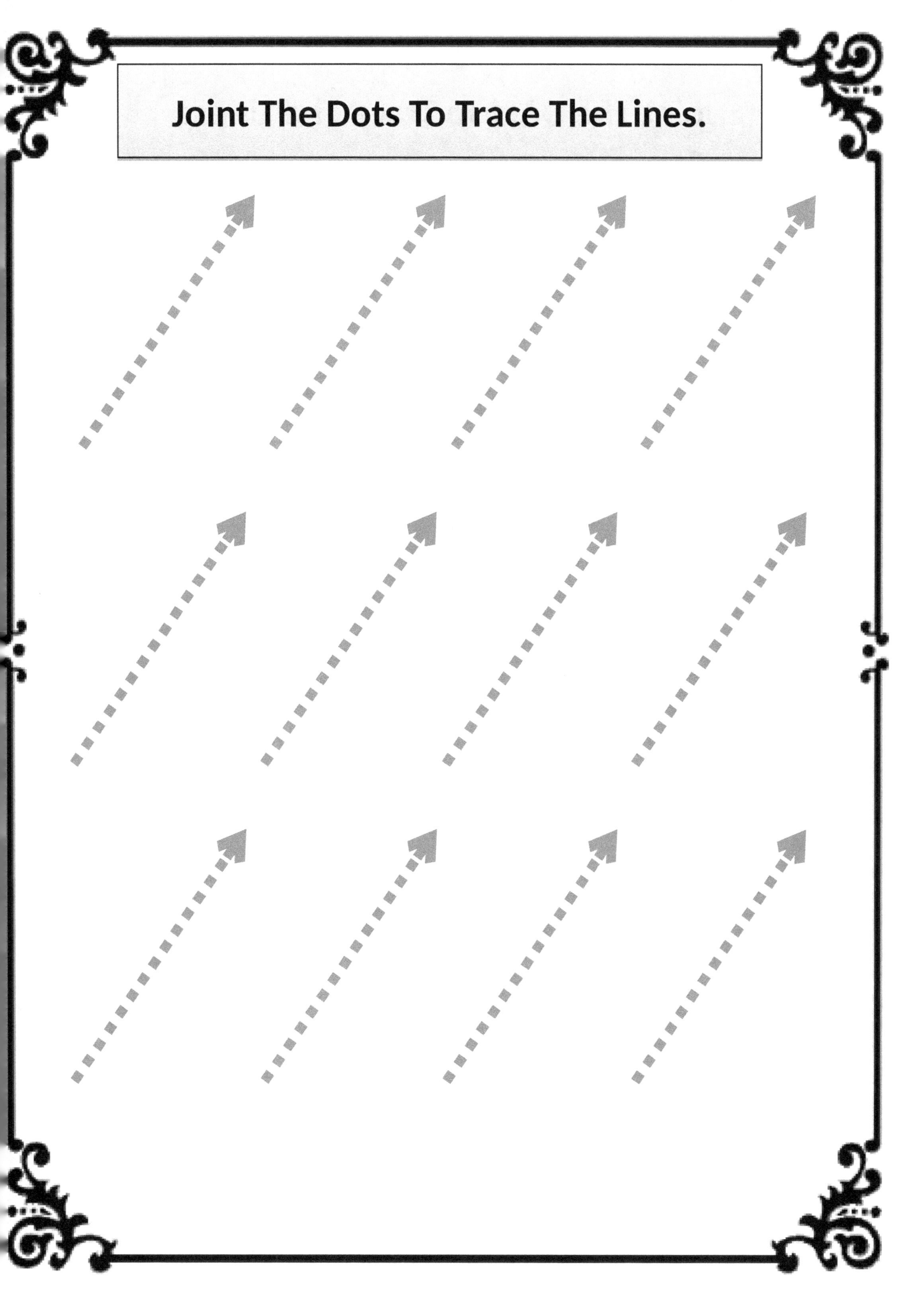

Joint The Dots To Trace The Lines.

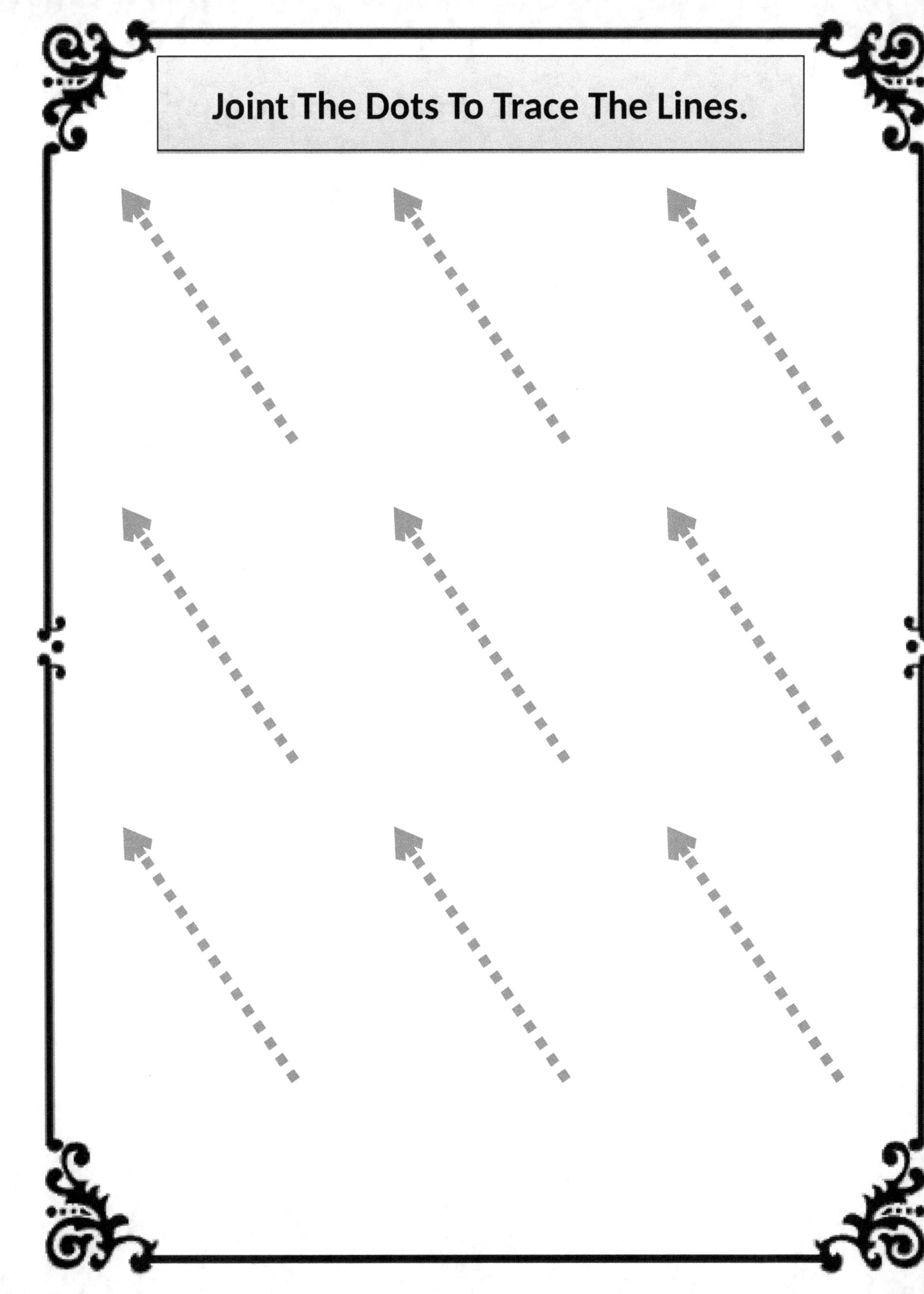

Joint The Dots To Trace The Lines.

Joint The Dots To Trace The Lines.

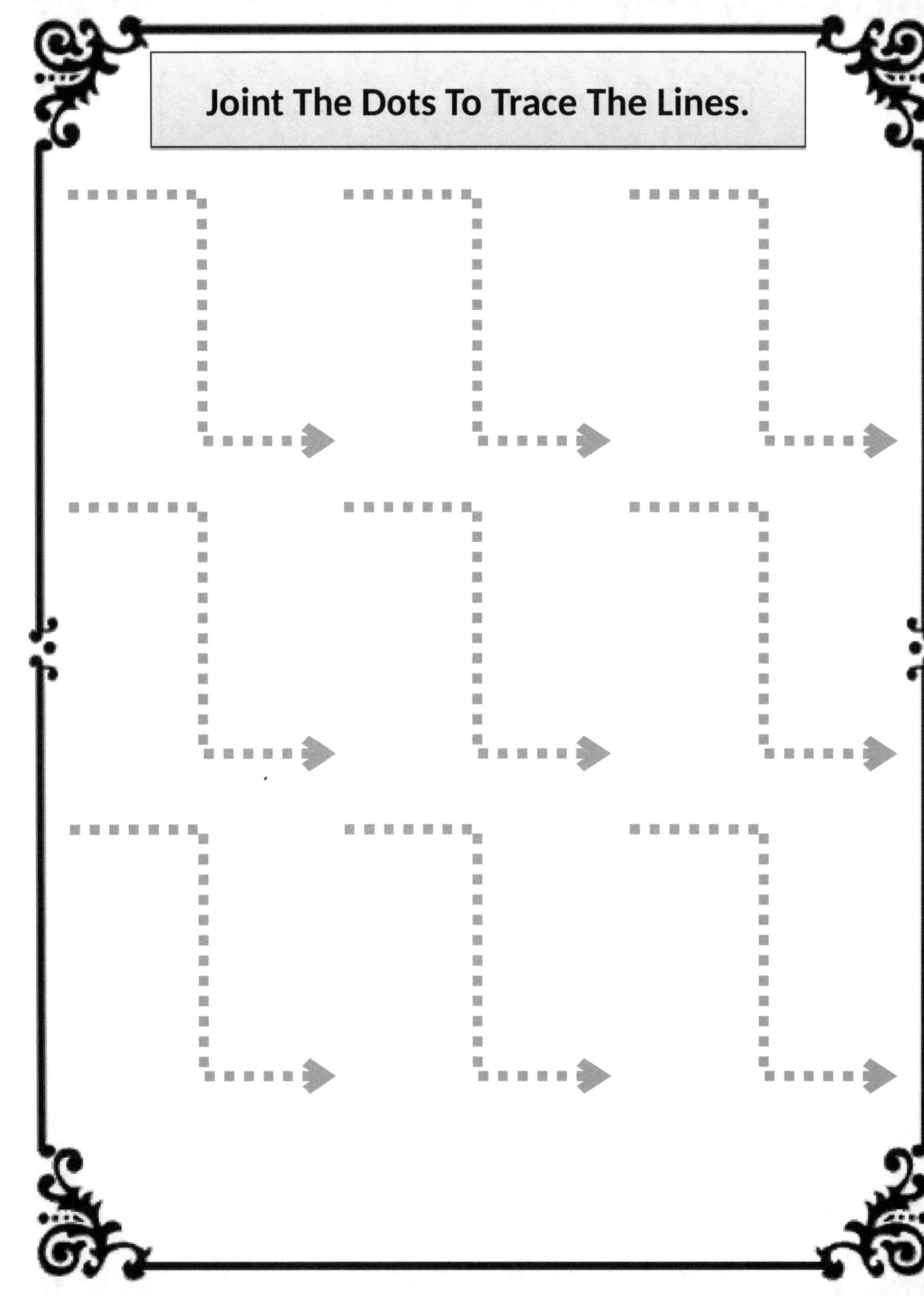

Joint The Dots To Trace The Lines.

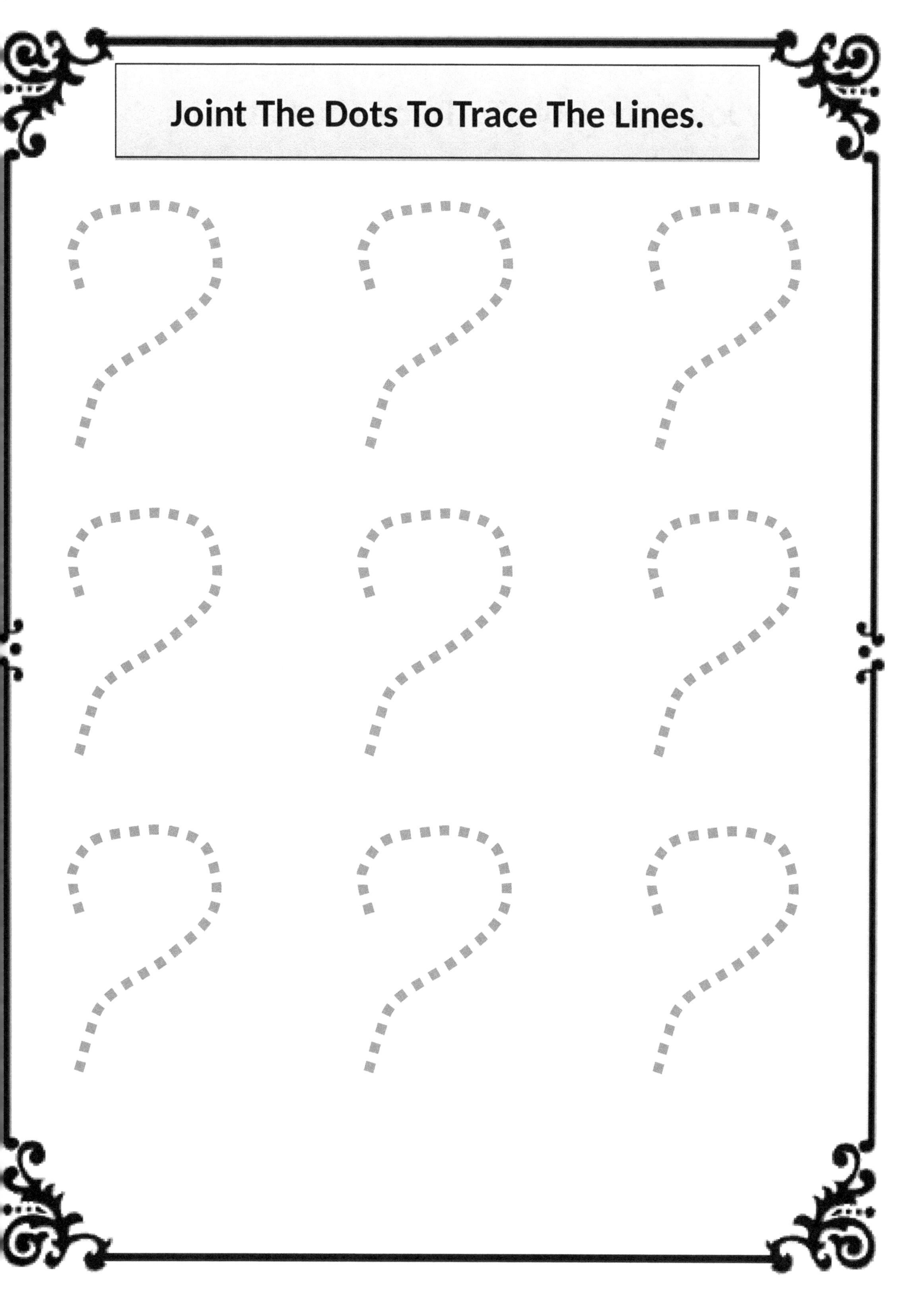

Joint The Dots To Trace The Patterns.

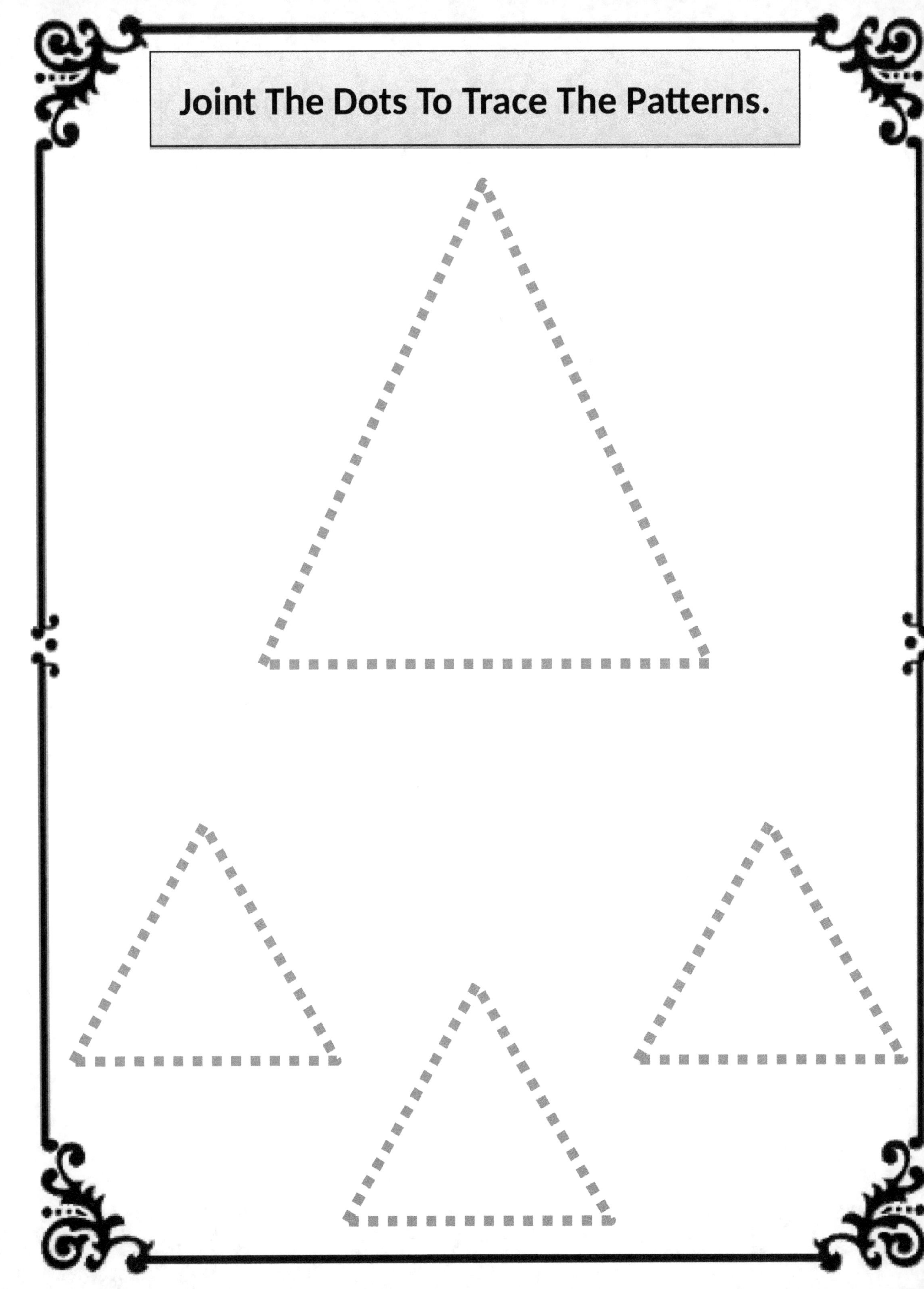

Joint The Dots To Trace The Patterns.

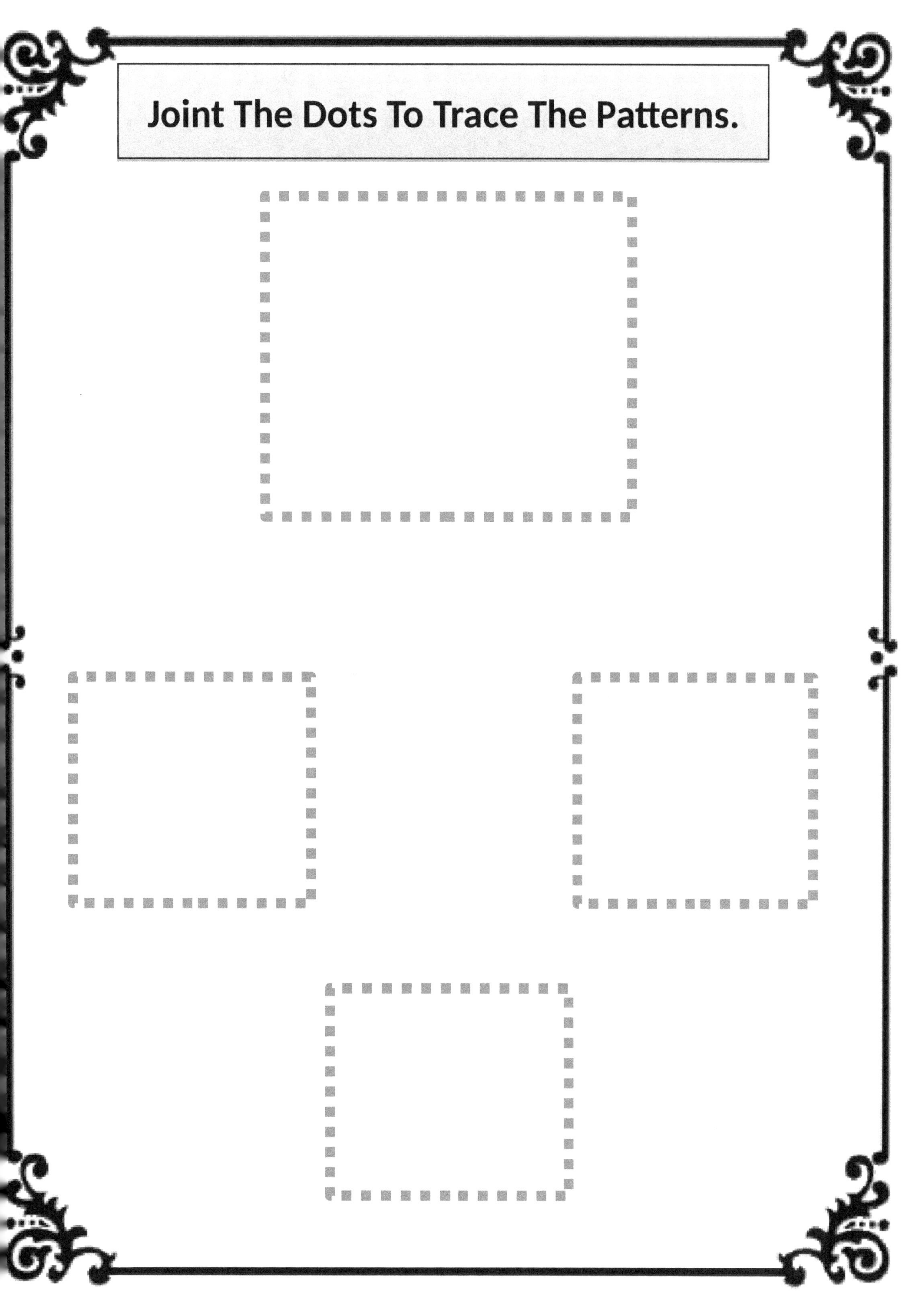

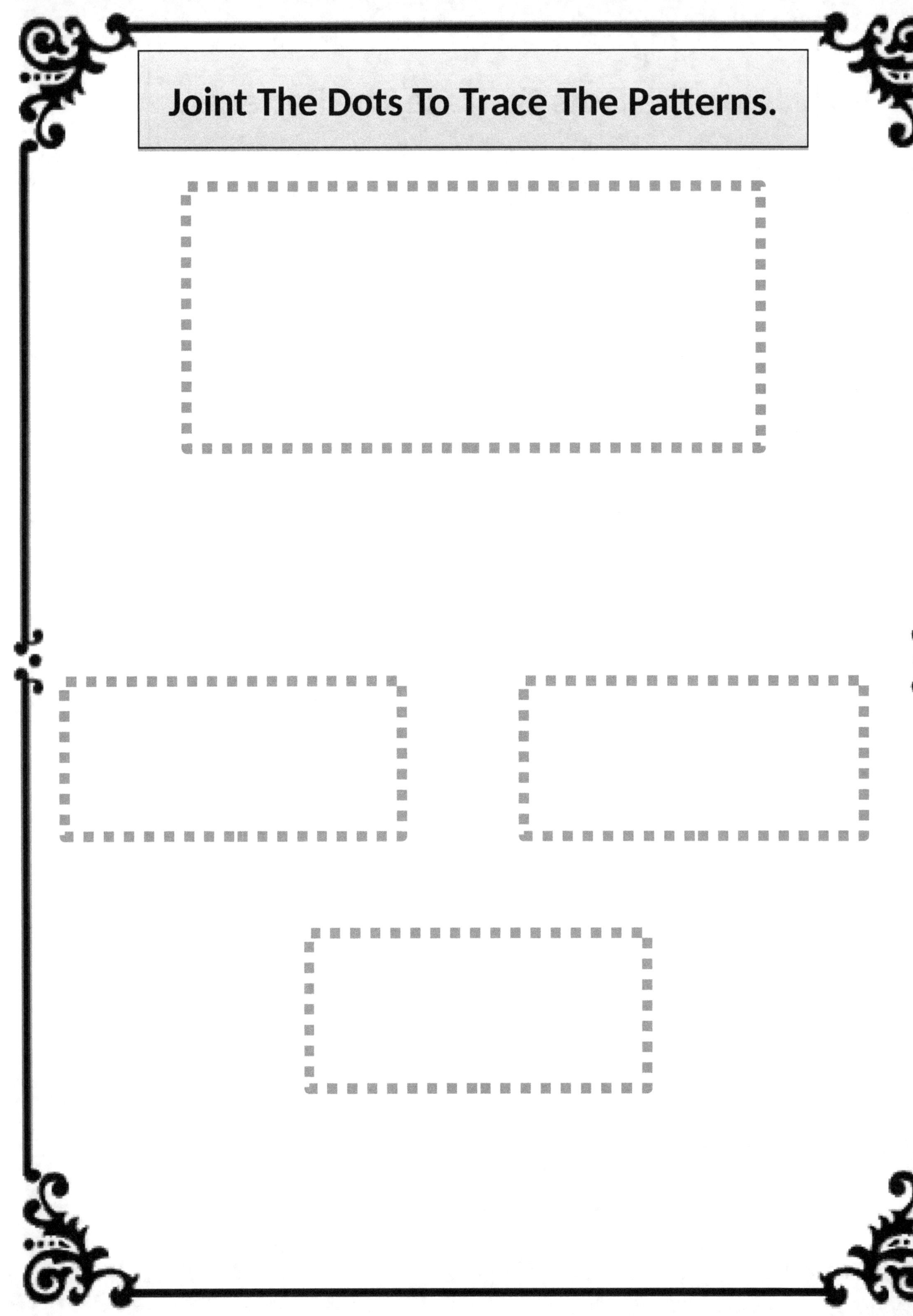

Joint The Dots To Trace The Patterns.

Joint The Dots To Trace The Patterns.

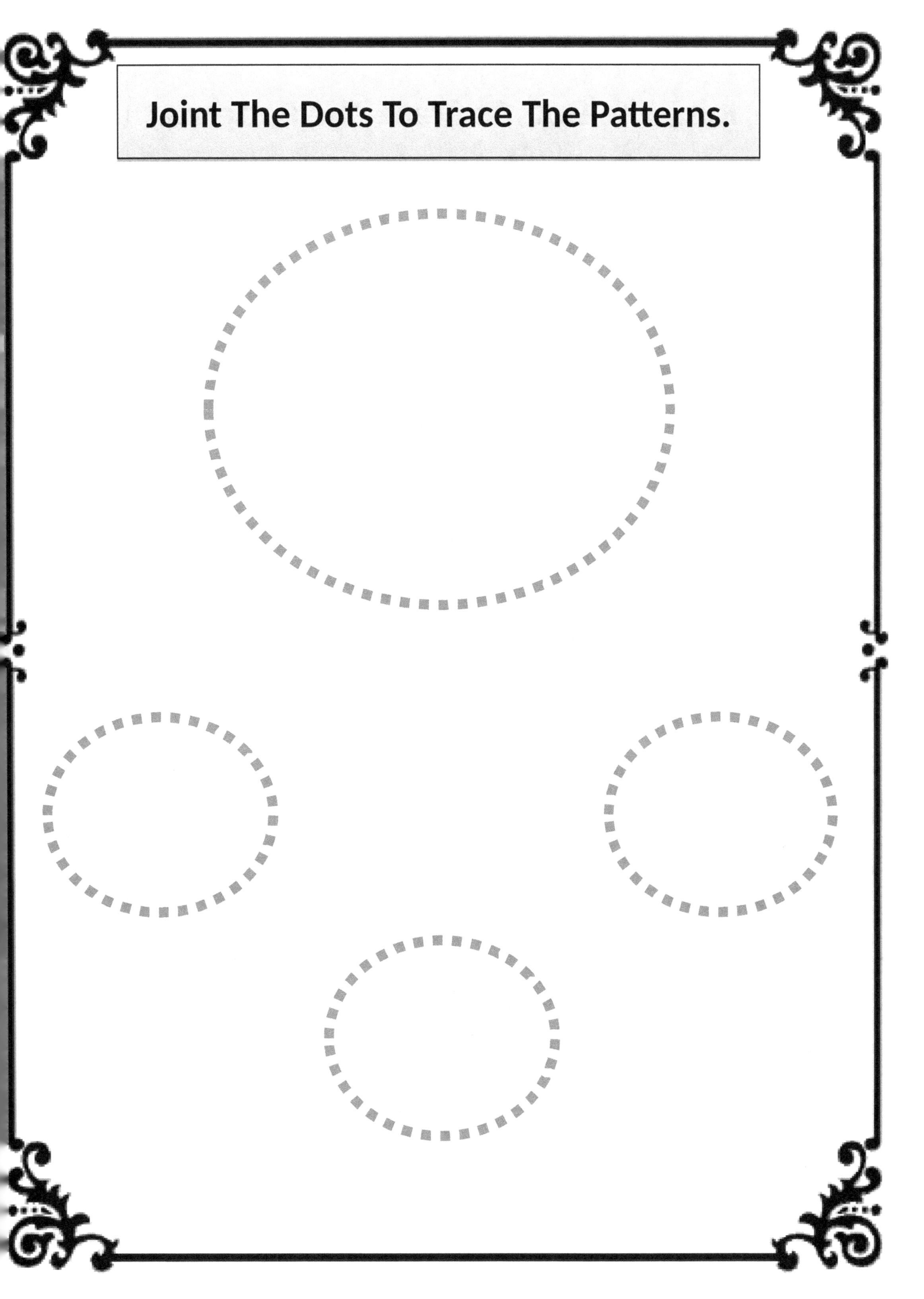

Joint The Dots To Trace The Patterns.

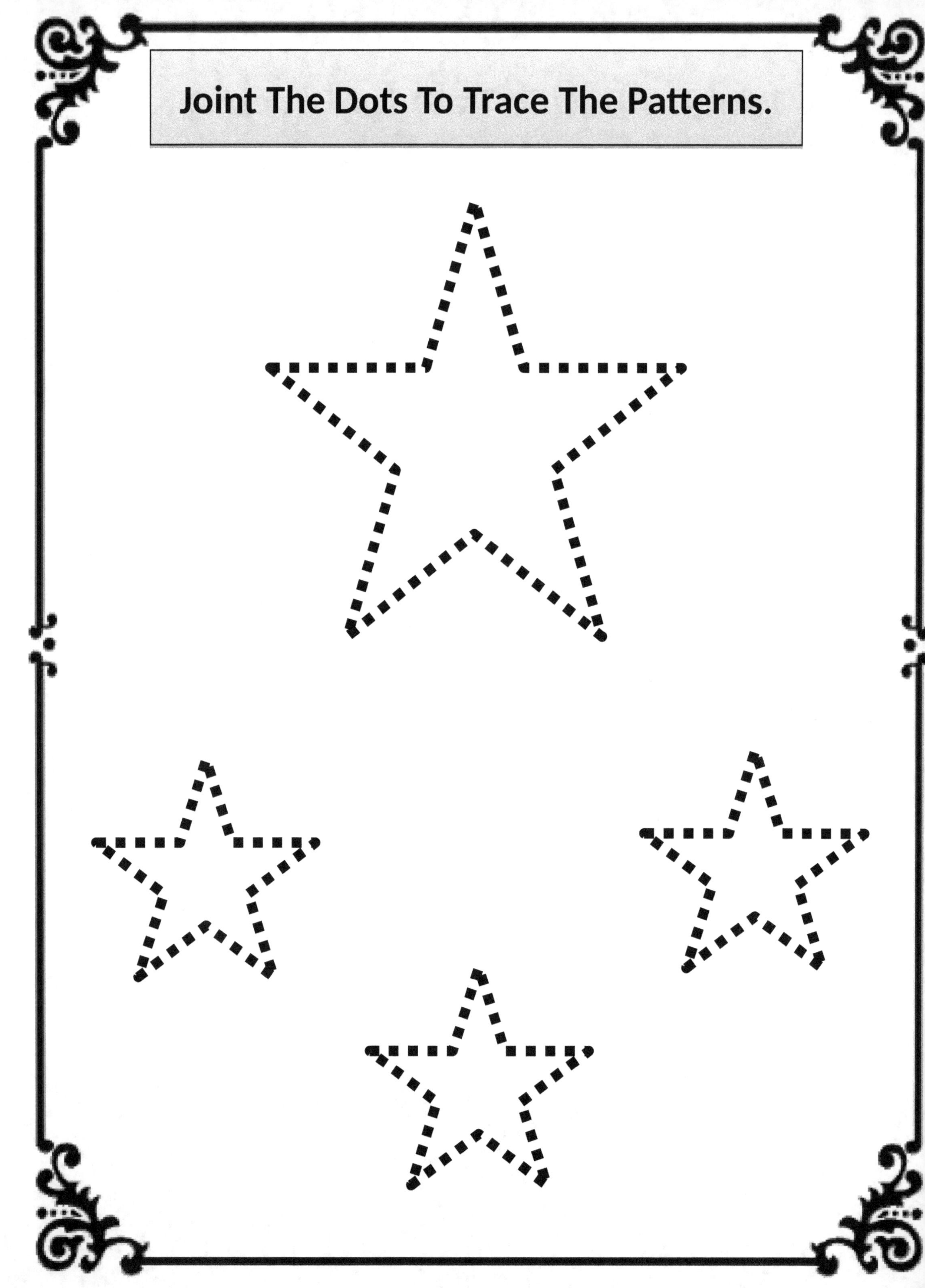

Joint The Dots To Trace The Patterns.

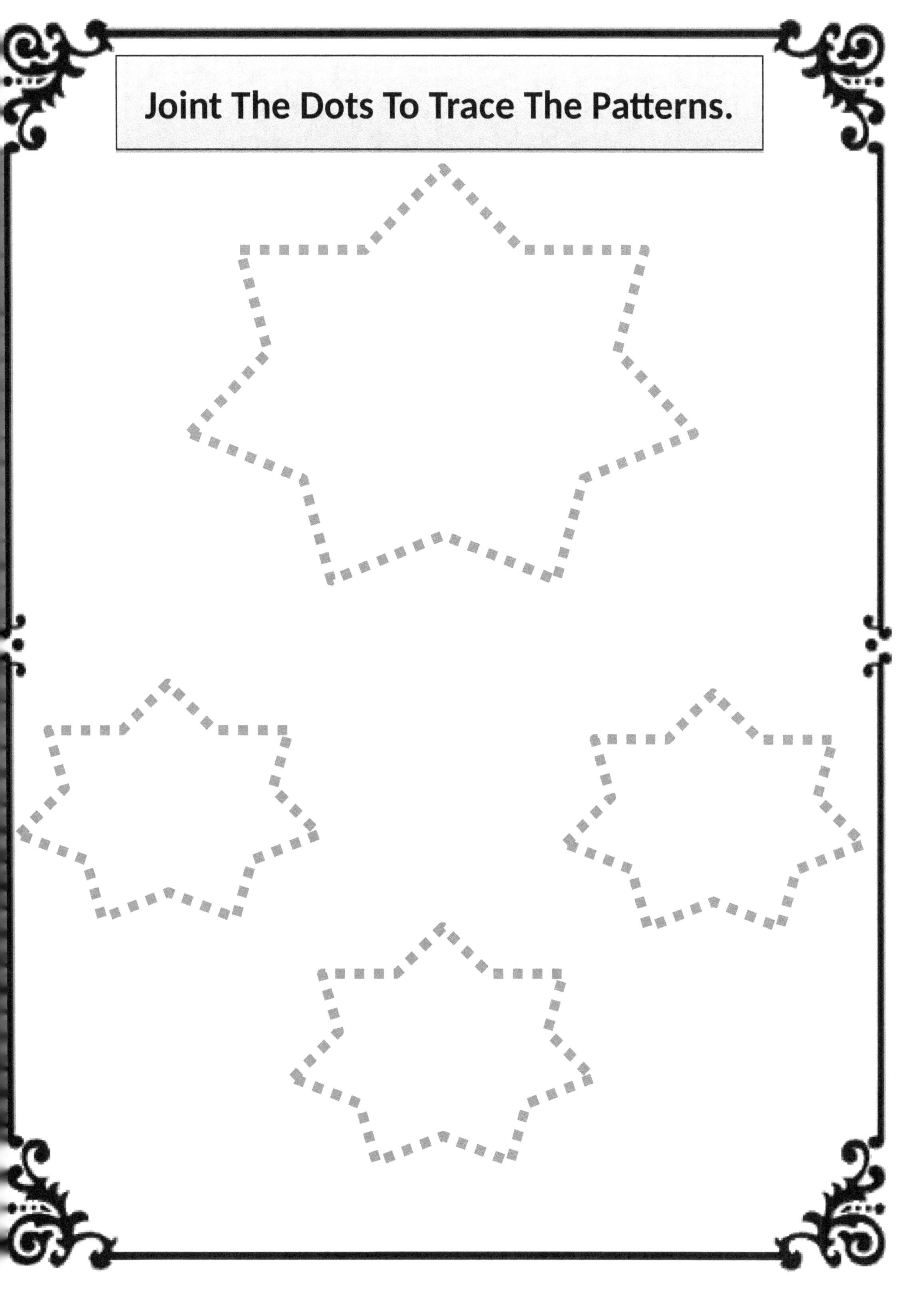

Joint The Dots To Trace The Patterns.

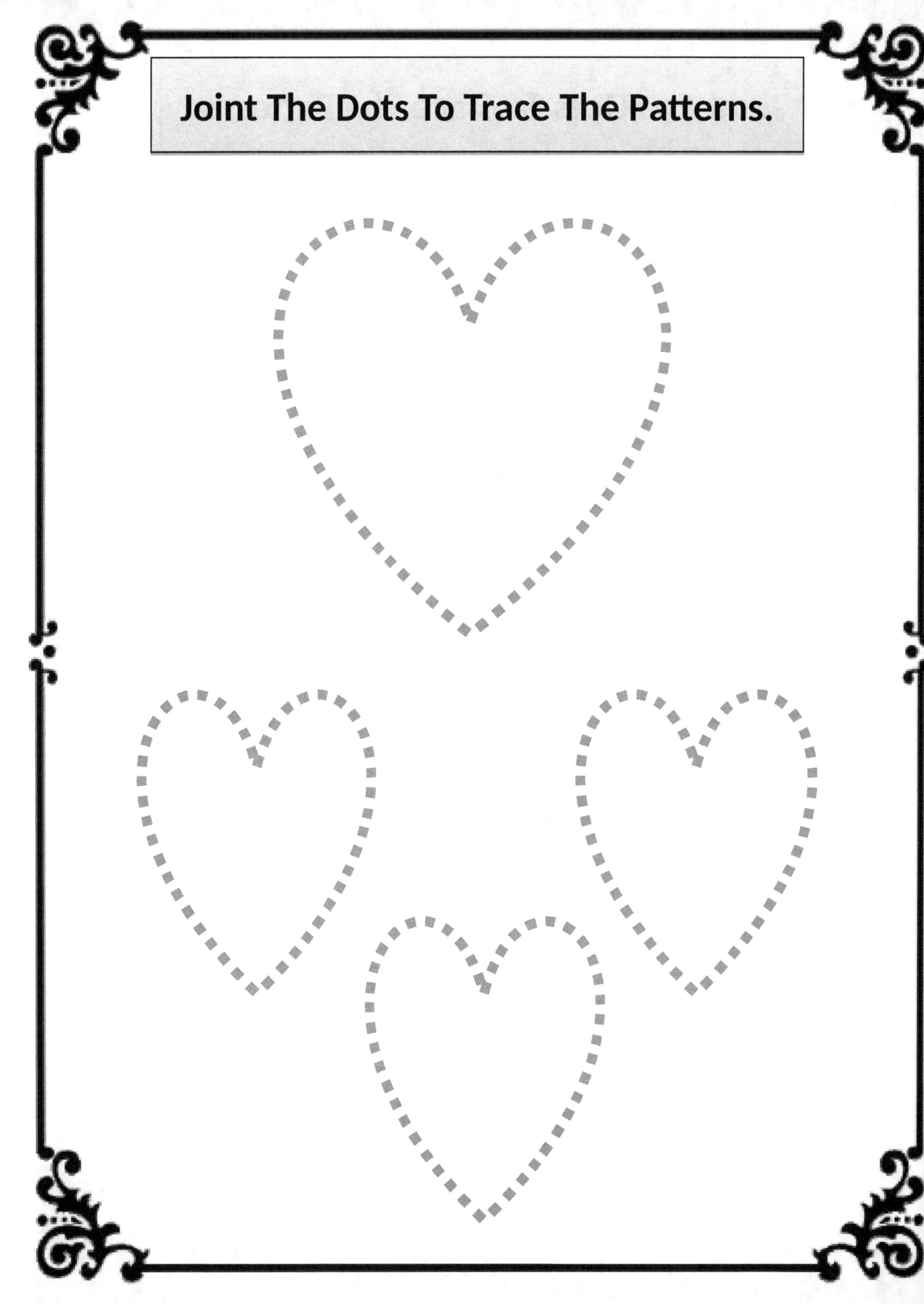

Joint The Dots To Trace The Lines.

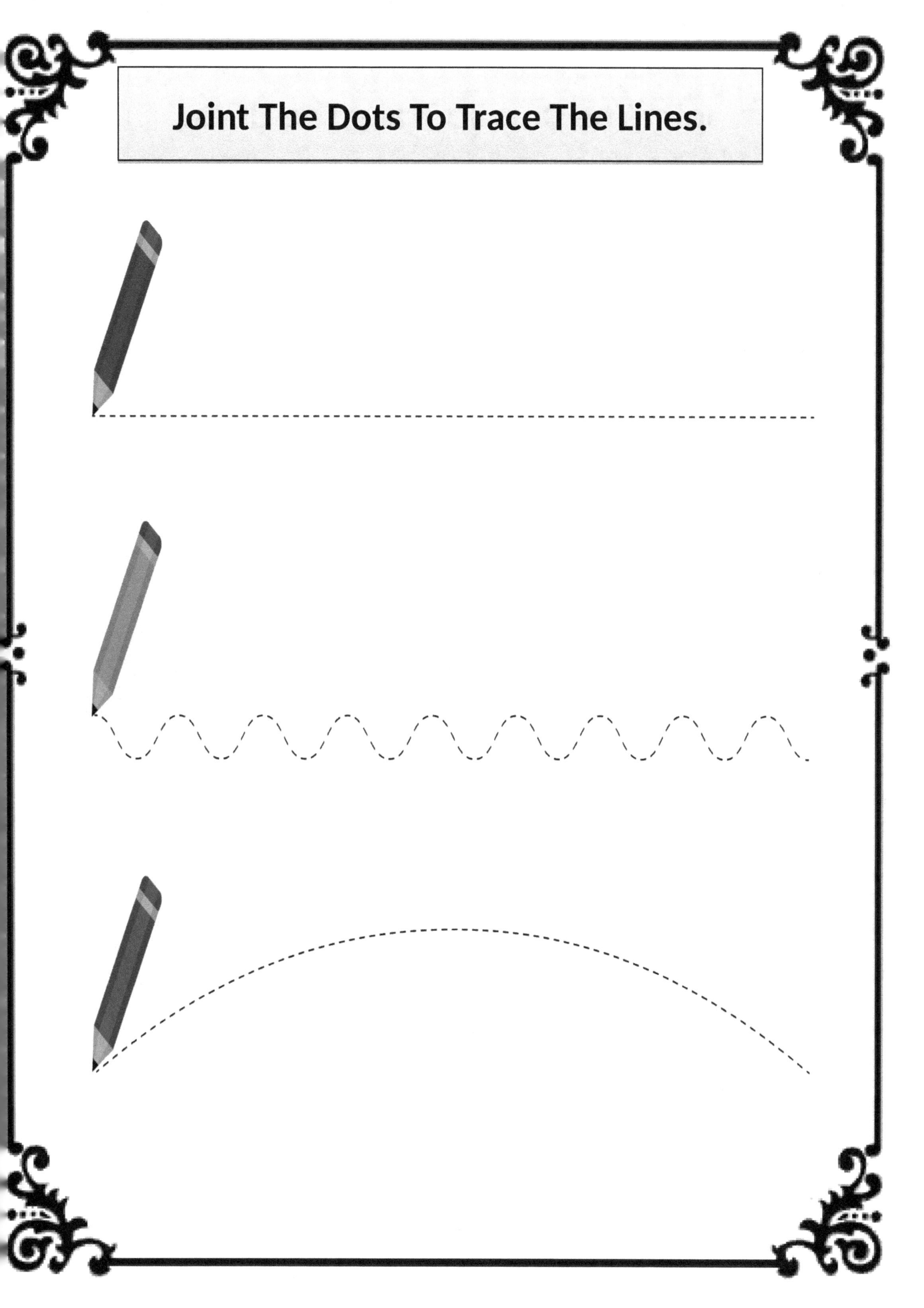

Joint The Dots To Trace The Lines.

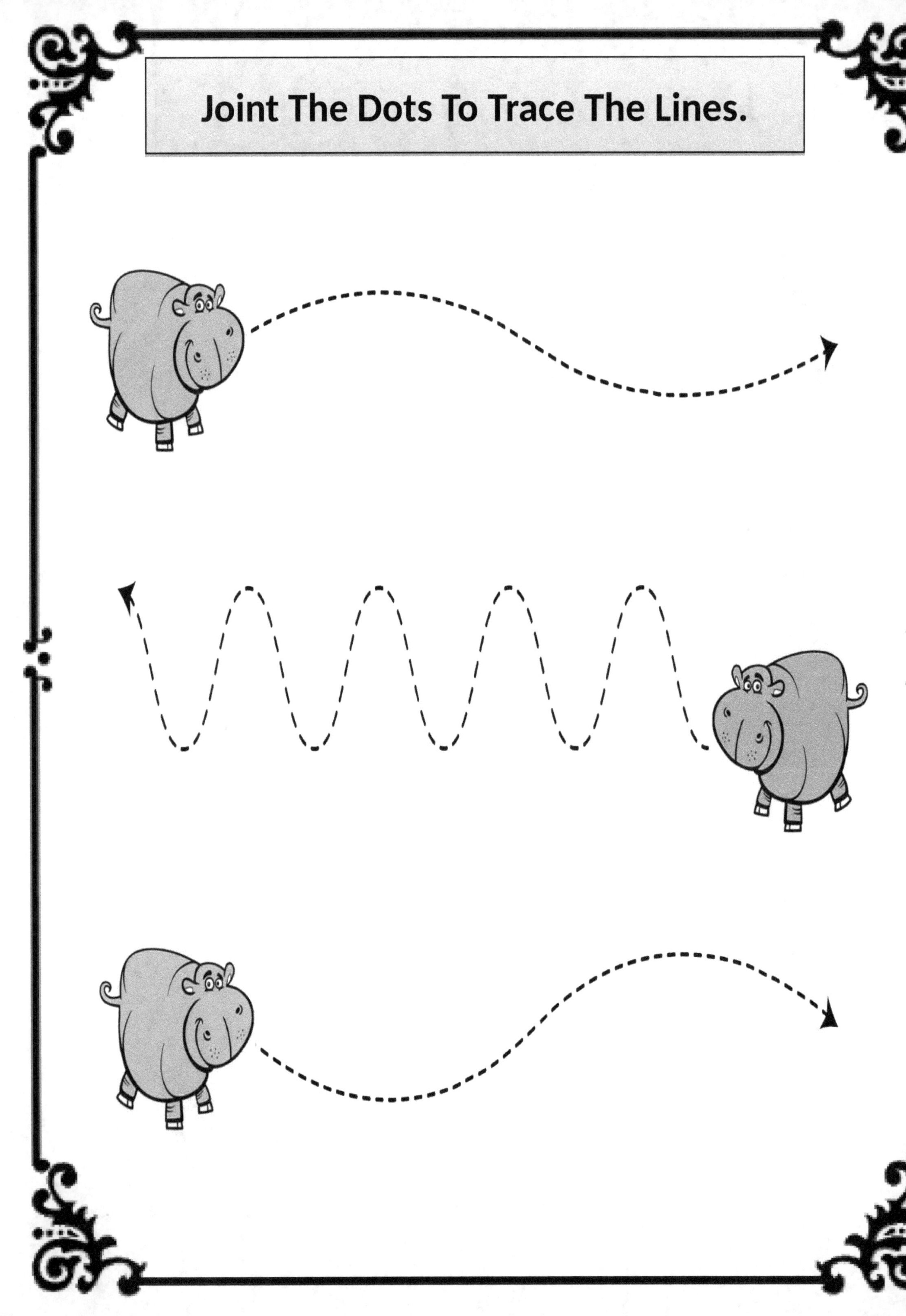

Joint The Dots To Trace The Lines.

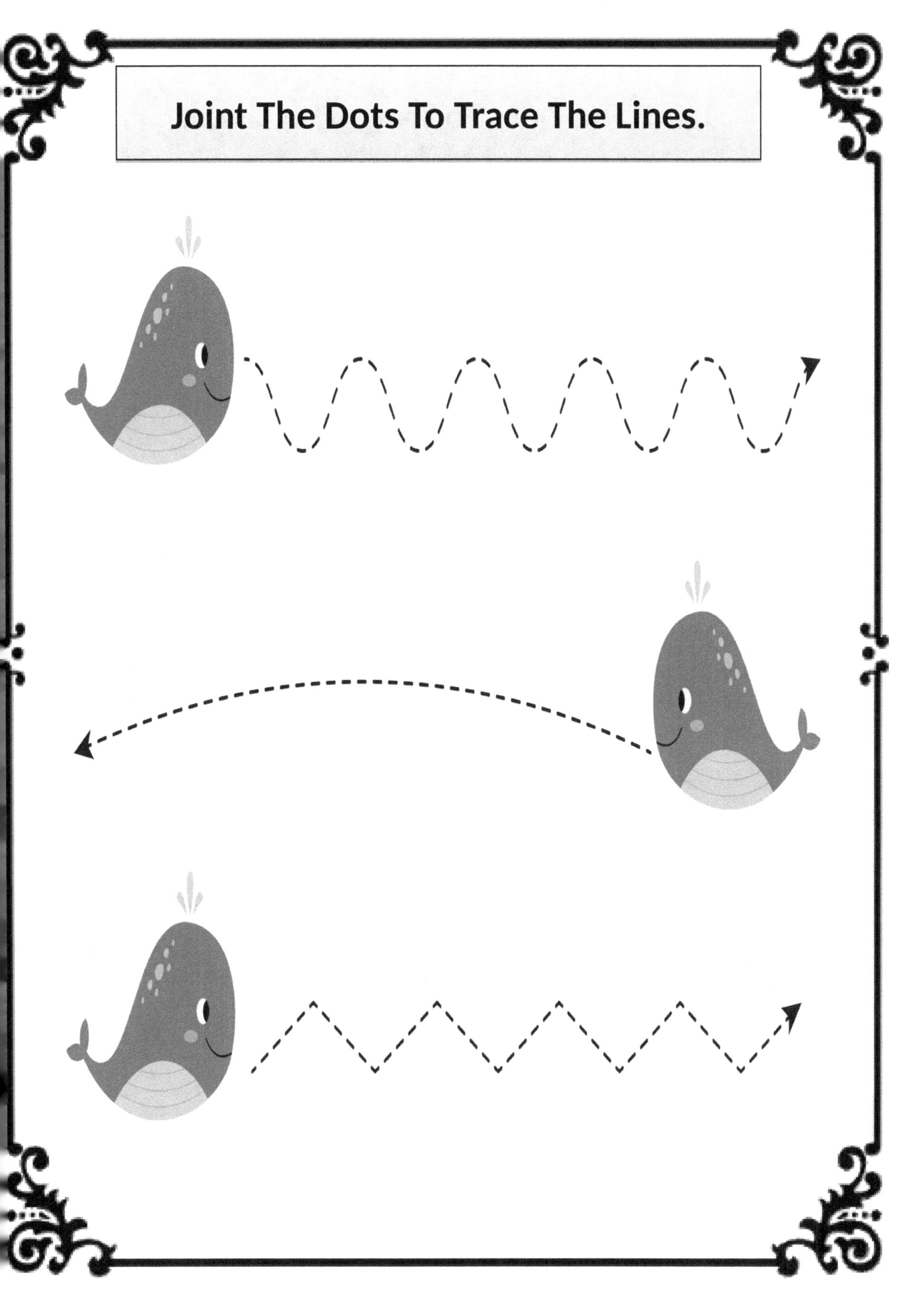

Joint The Dots To Trace The Lines.

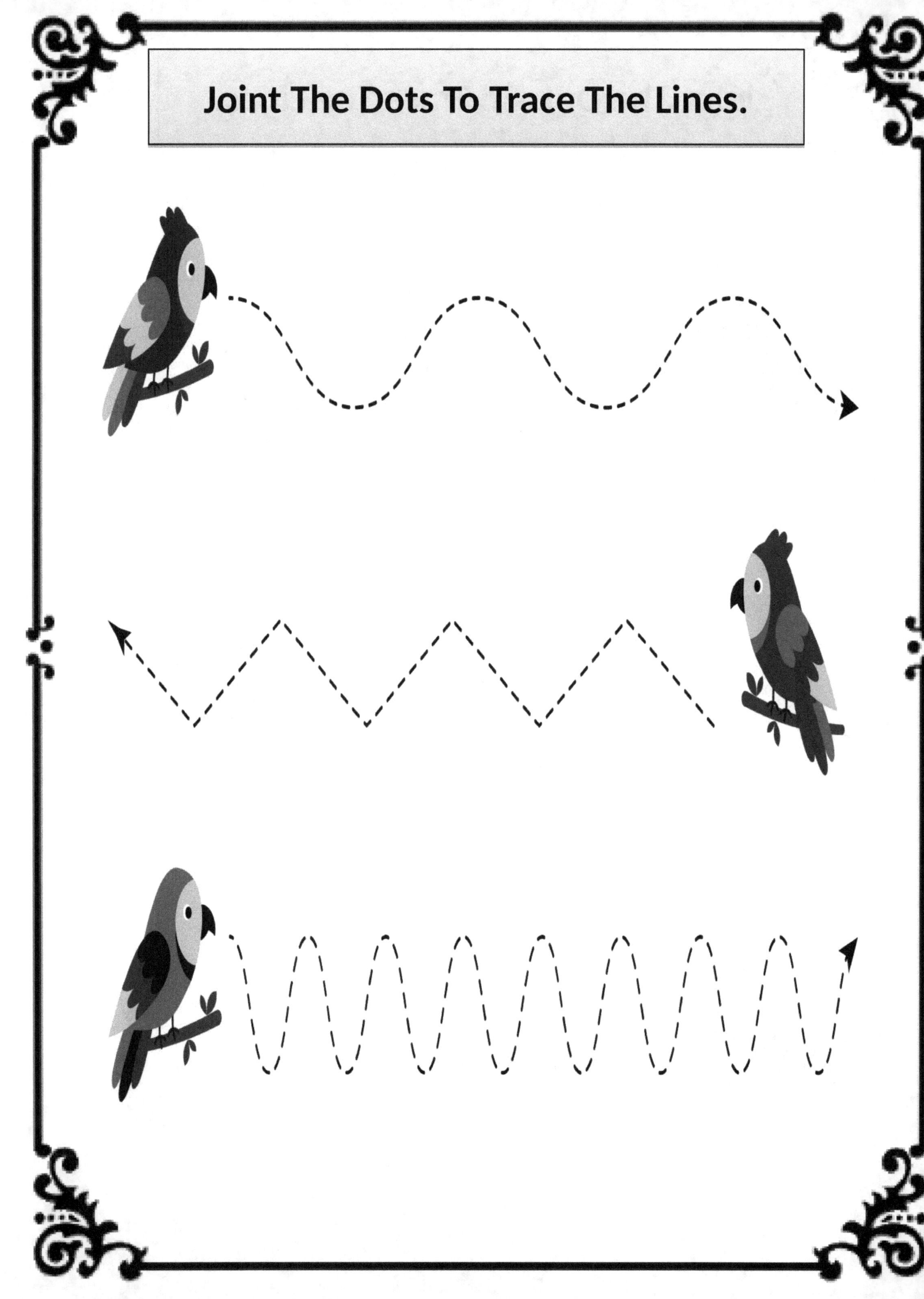

Joint The Dots To Trace The Lines.

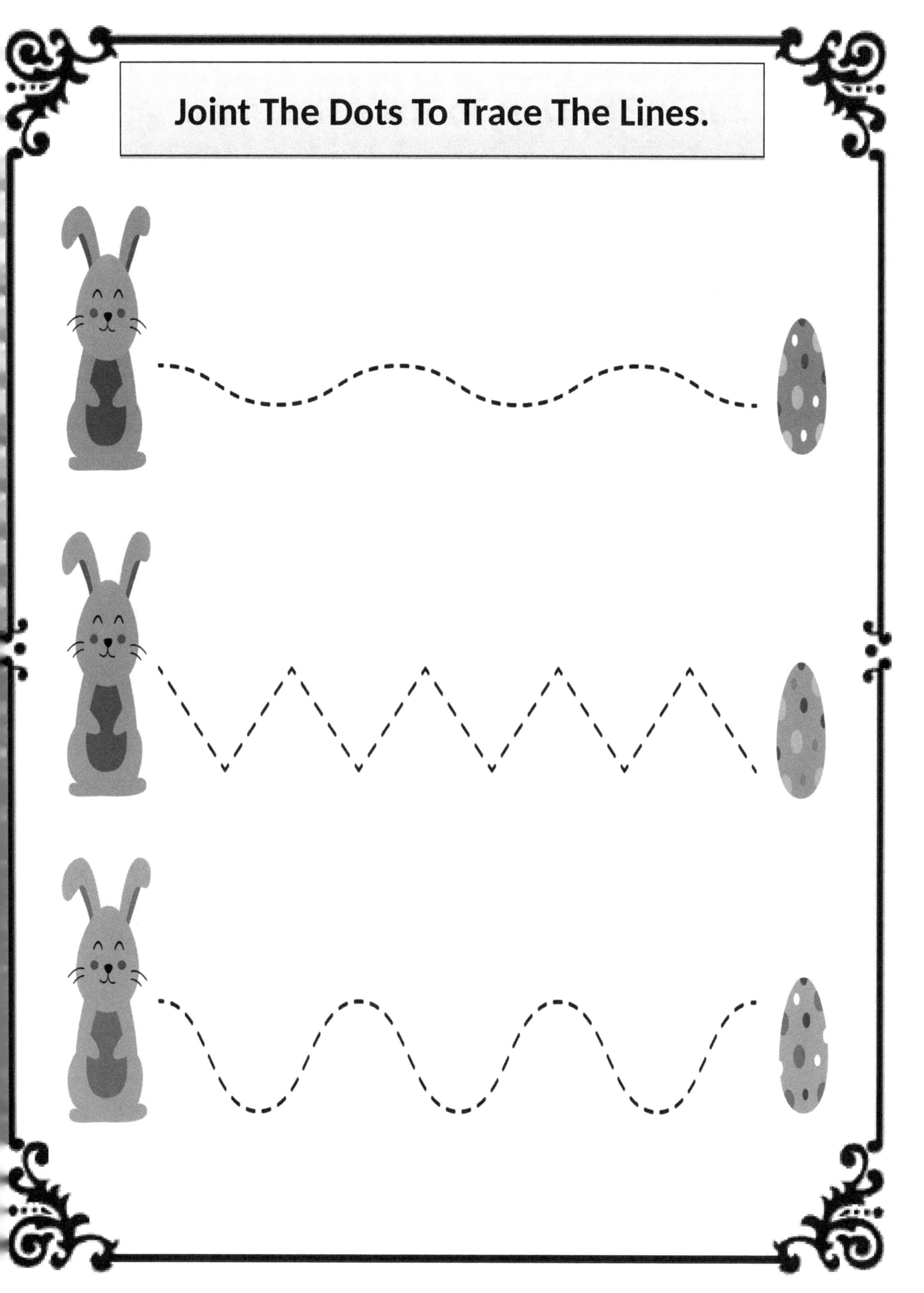

Joint The Dots To Trace The Lines.

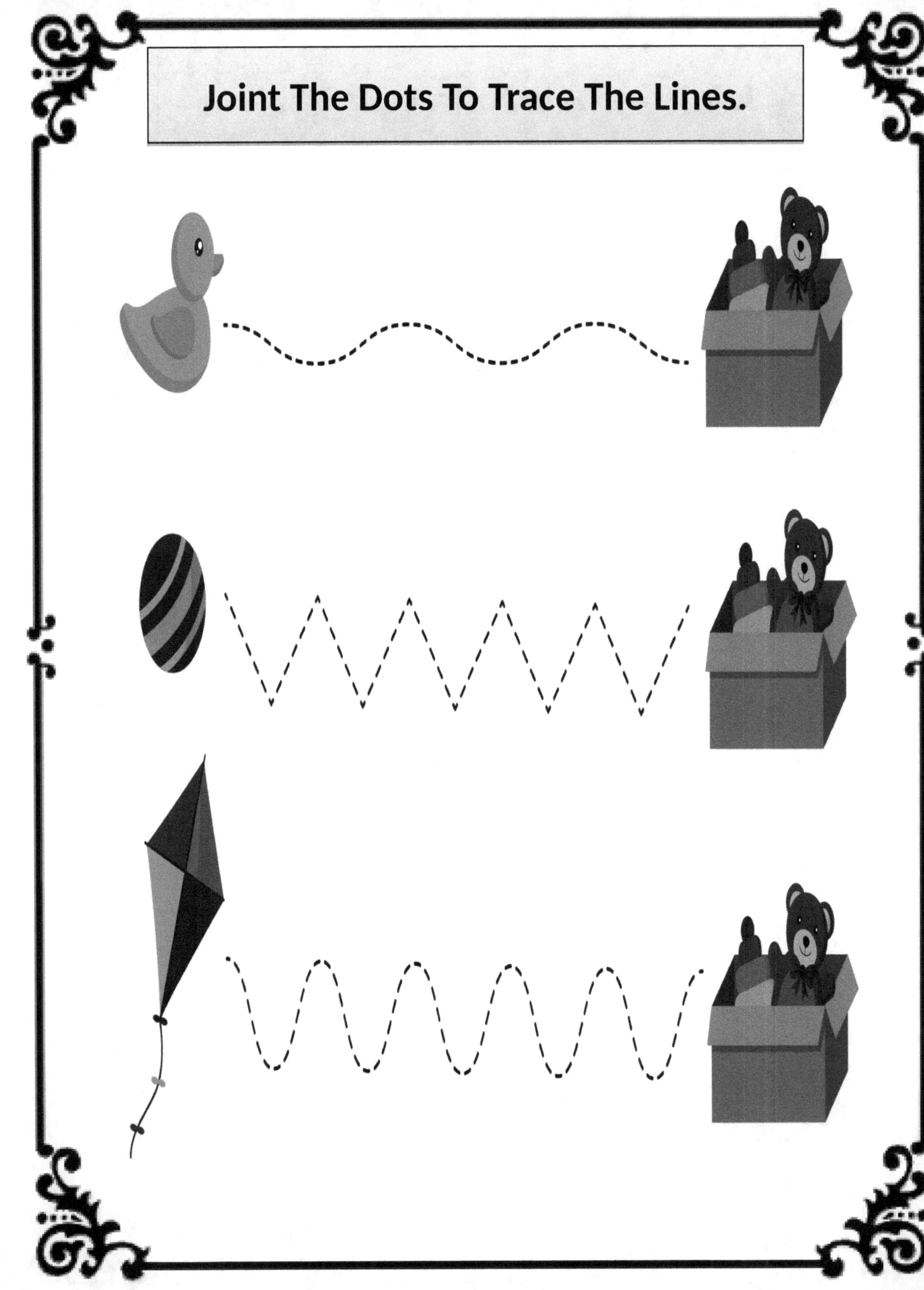

Joint The Dots To Trace The Lines.

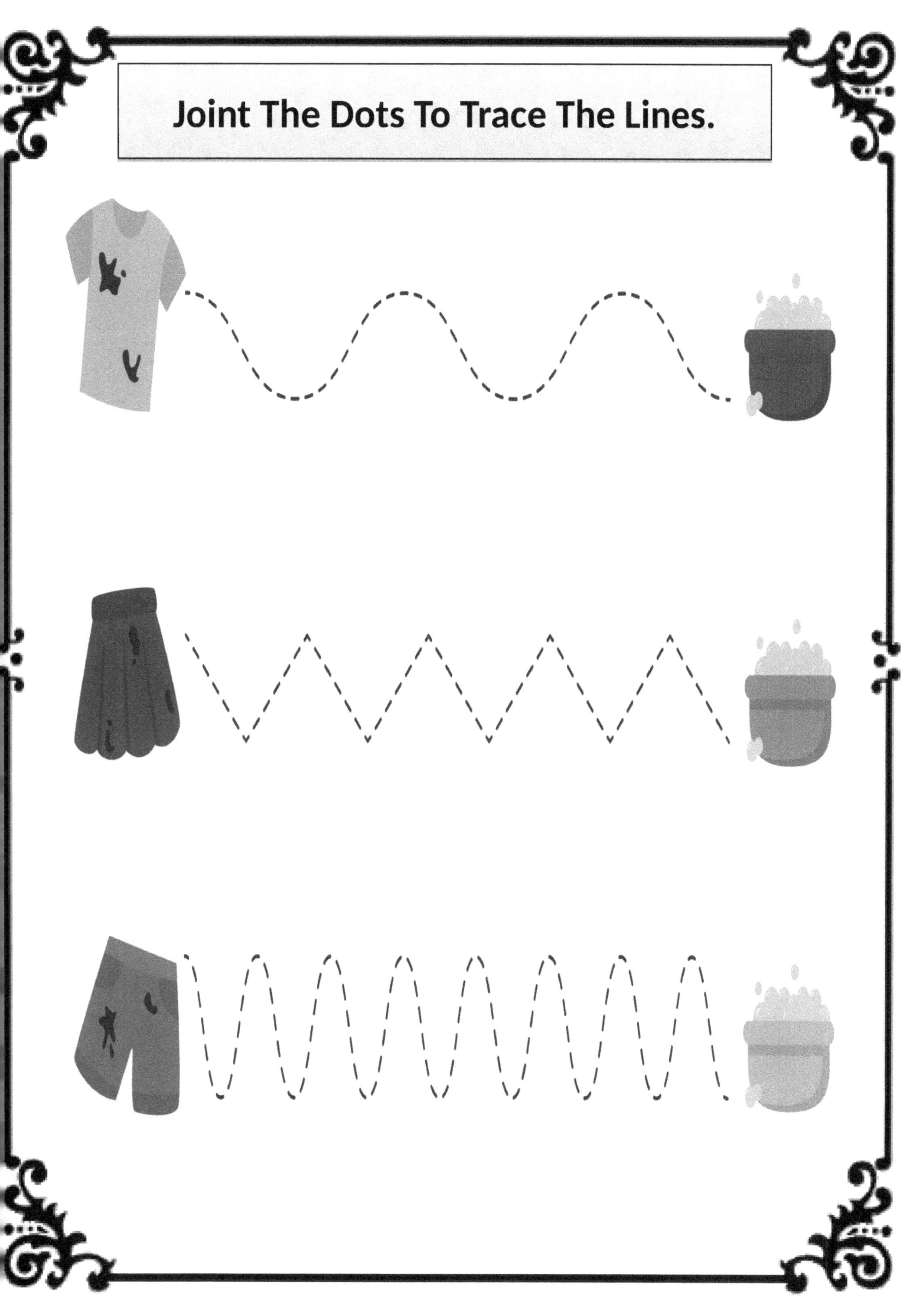

Joint The Dots To Trace The Lines.

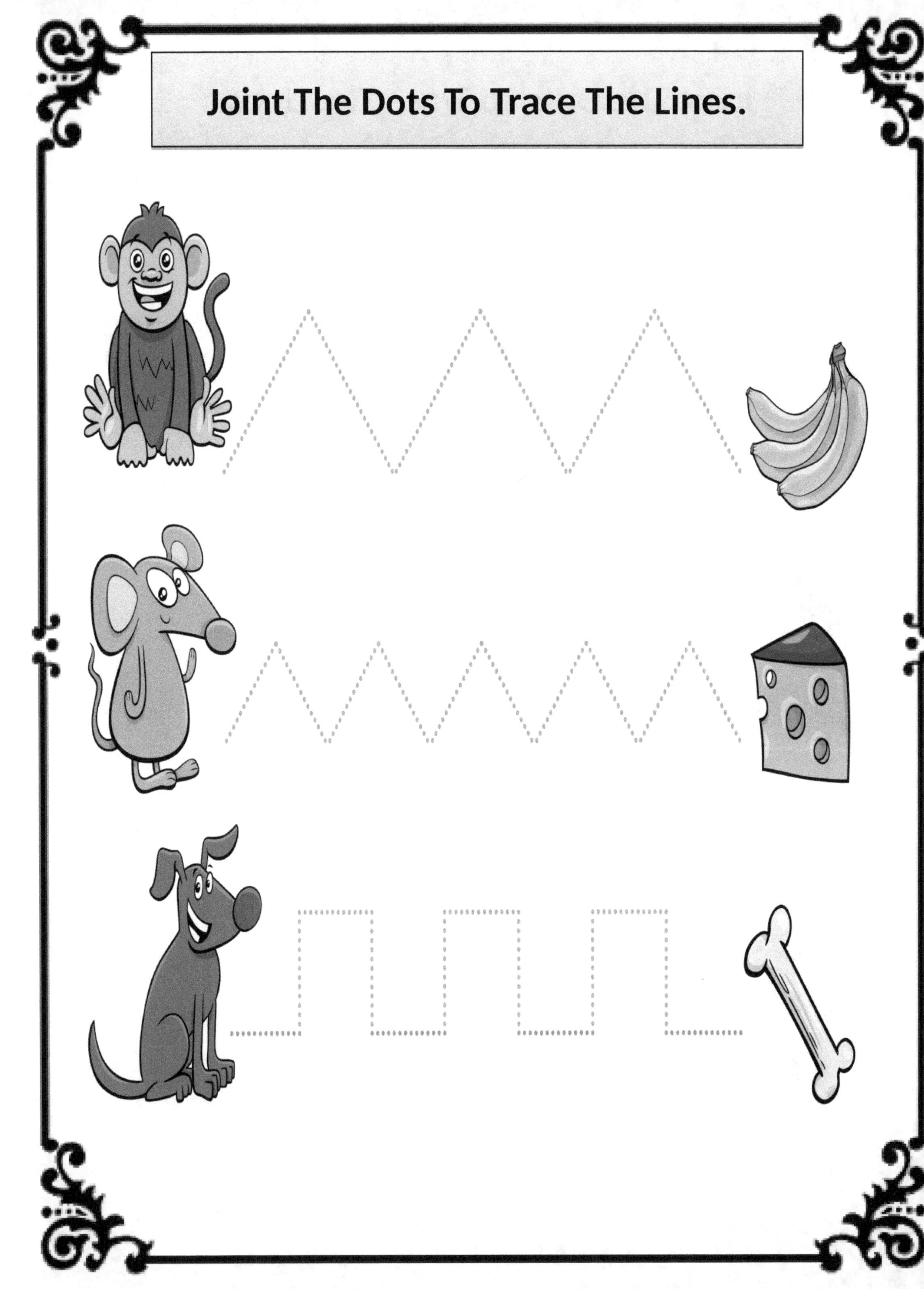

Joint The Dots To Trace The Lines.

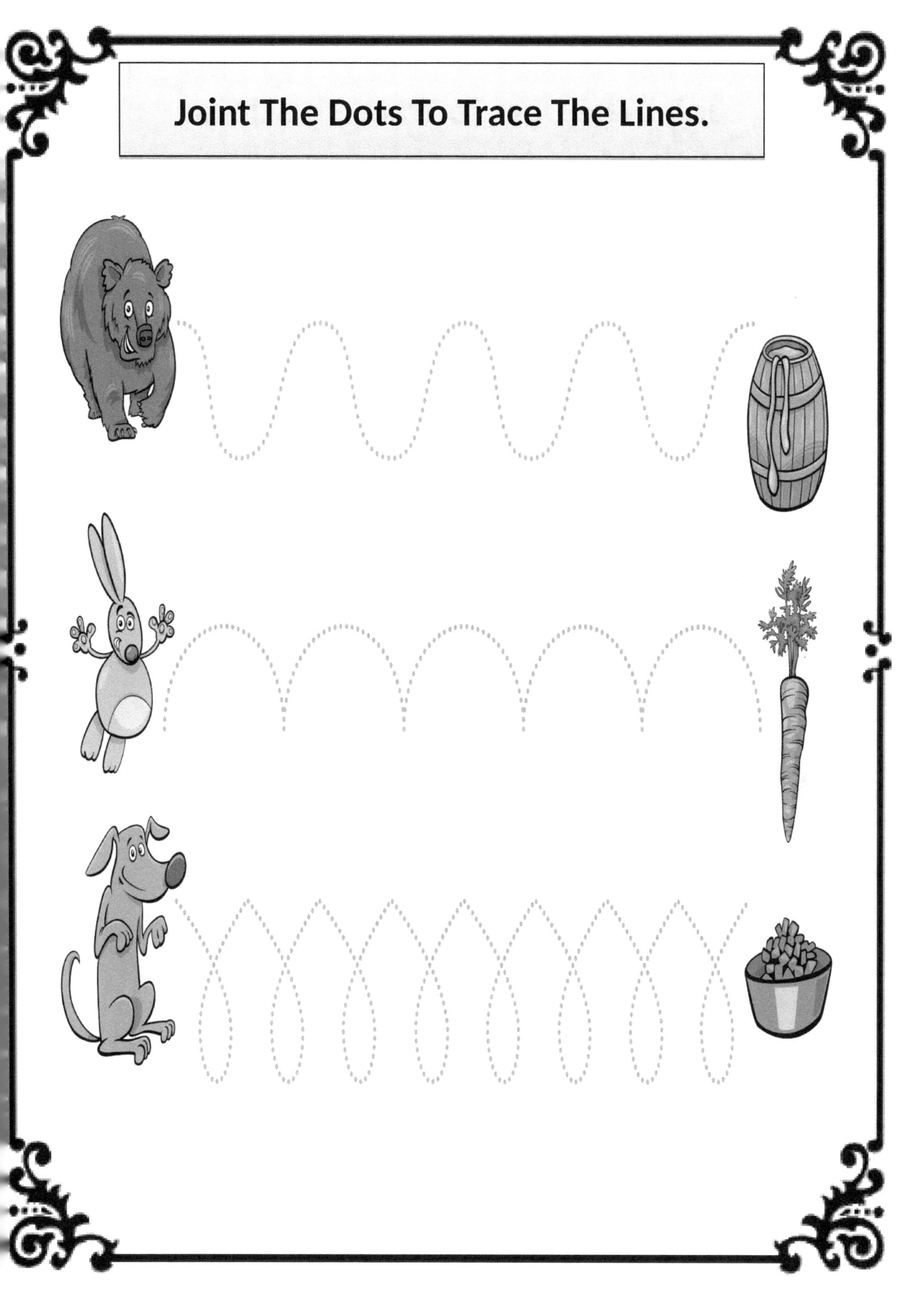

Joint The Dots To Trace The Lines.

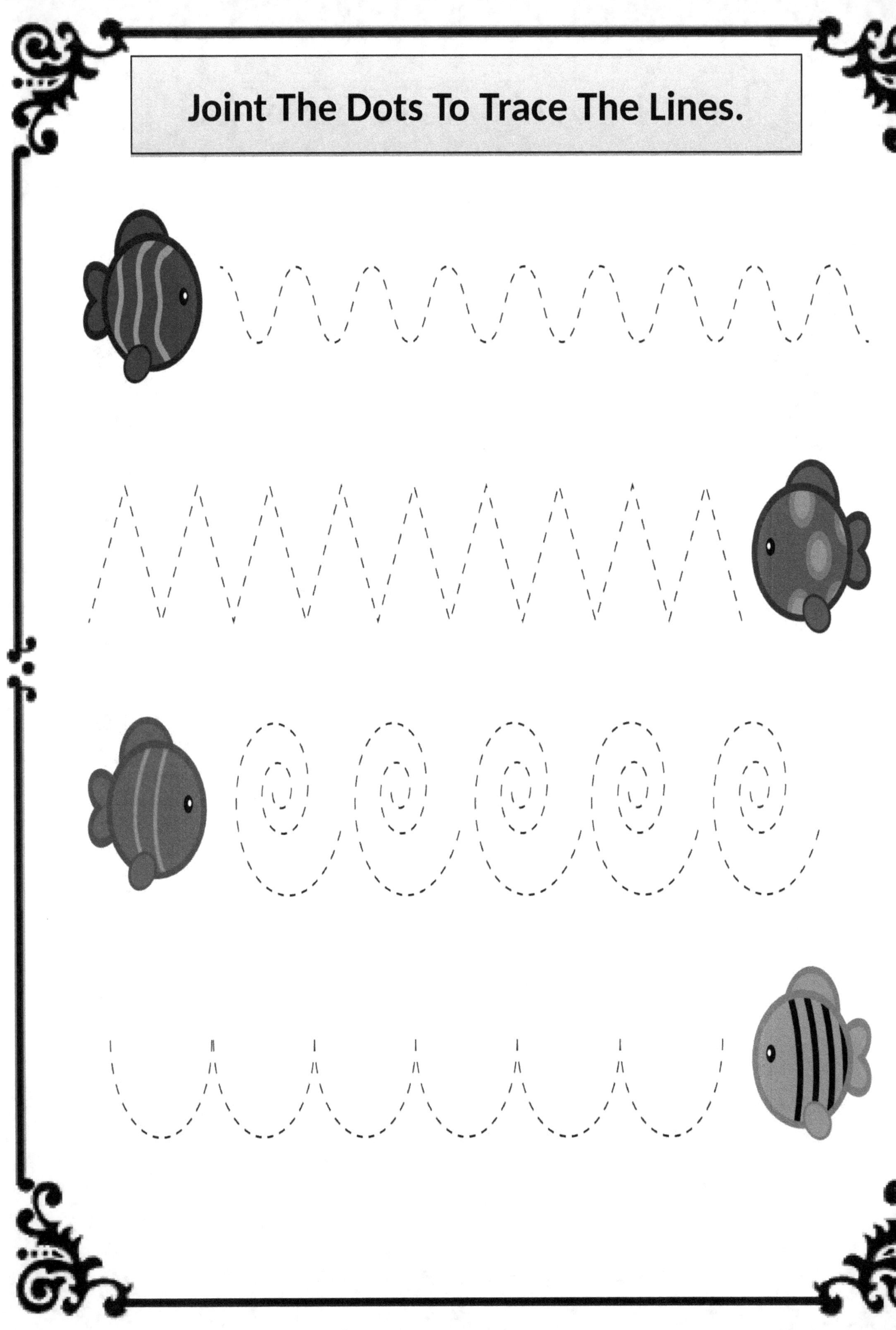

Trace The Letters

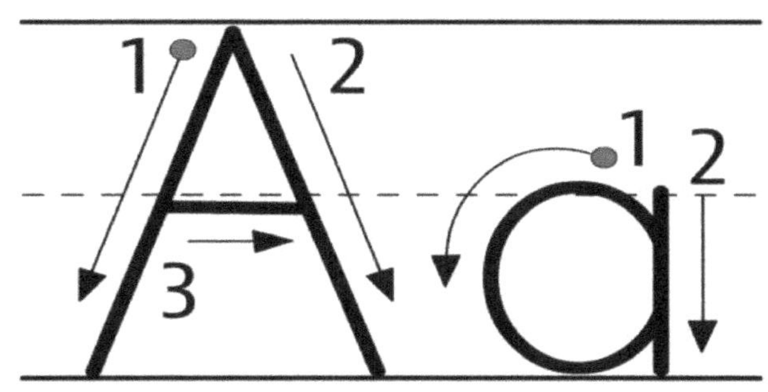

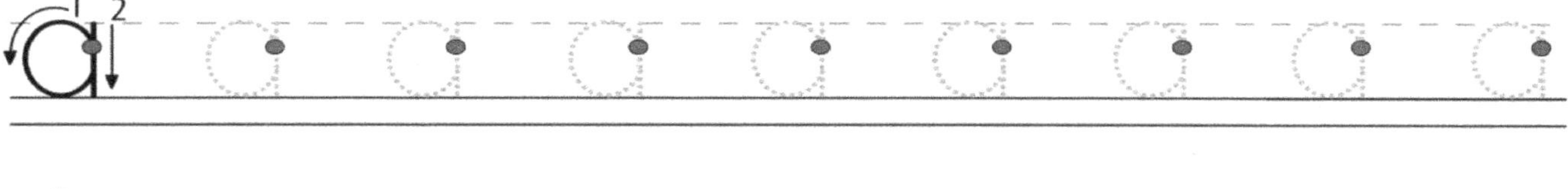

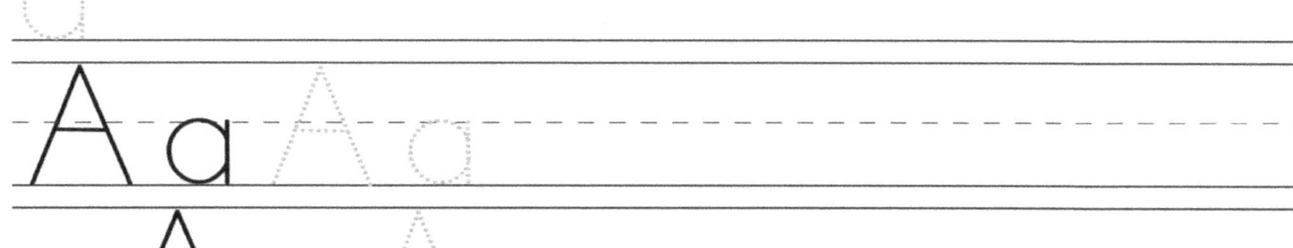

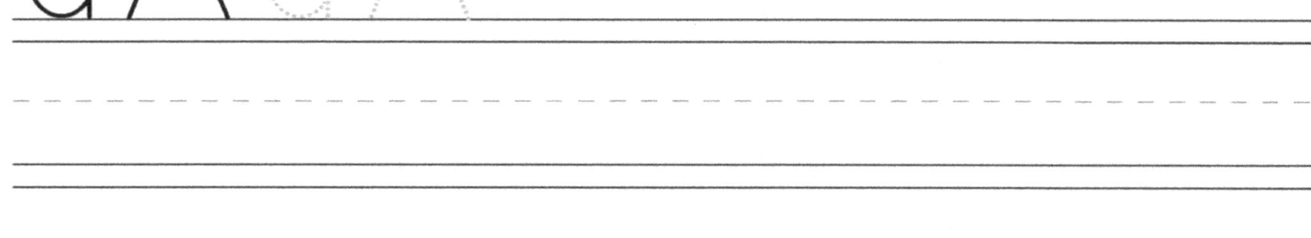

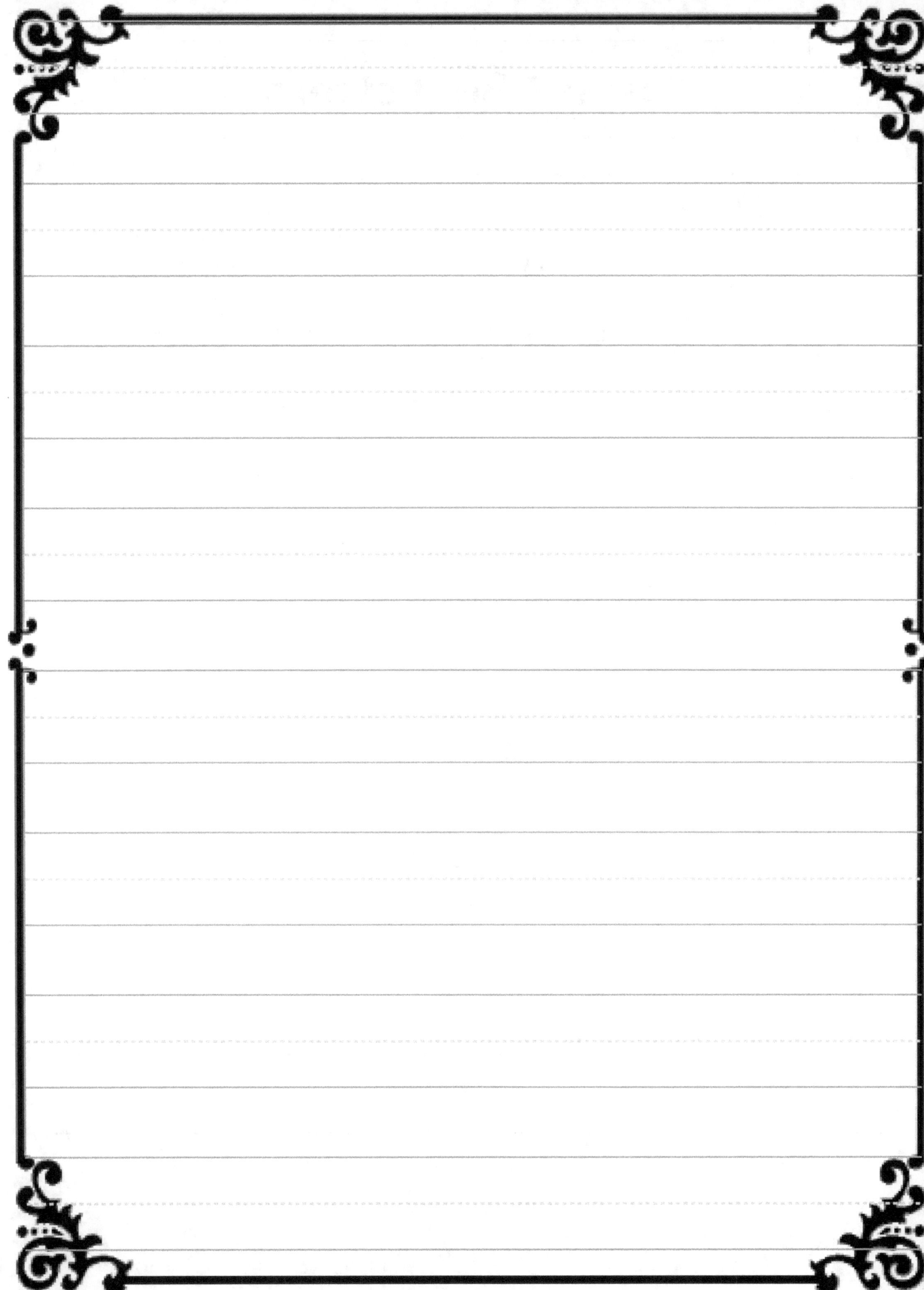

Trace The Letters

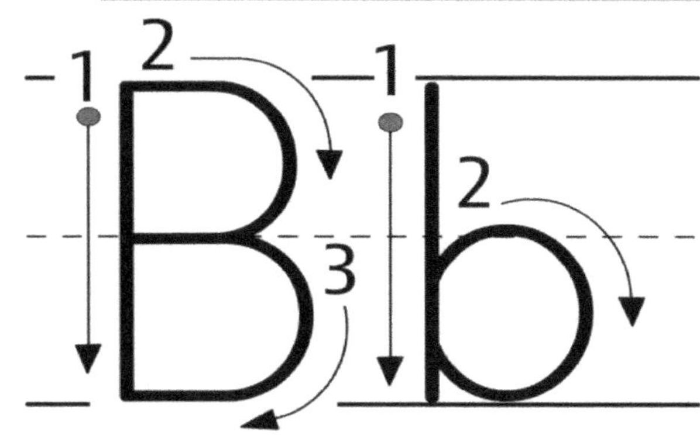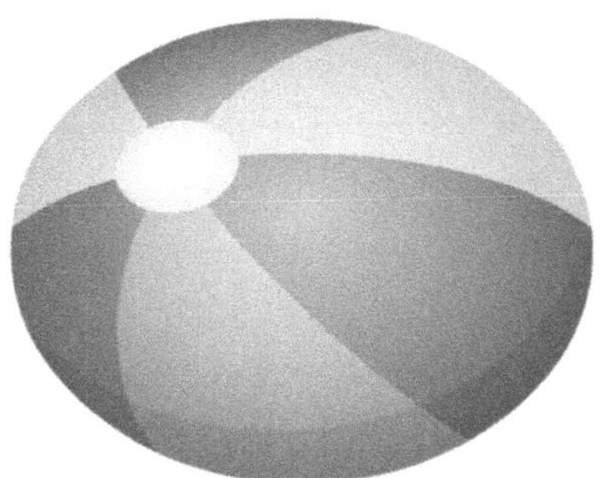

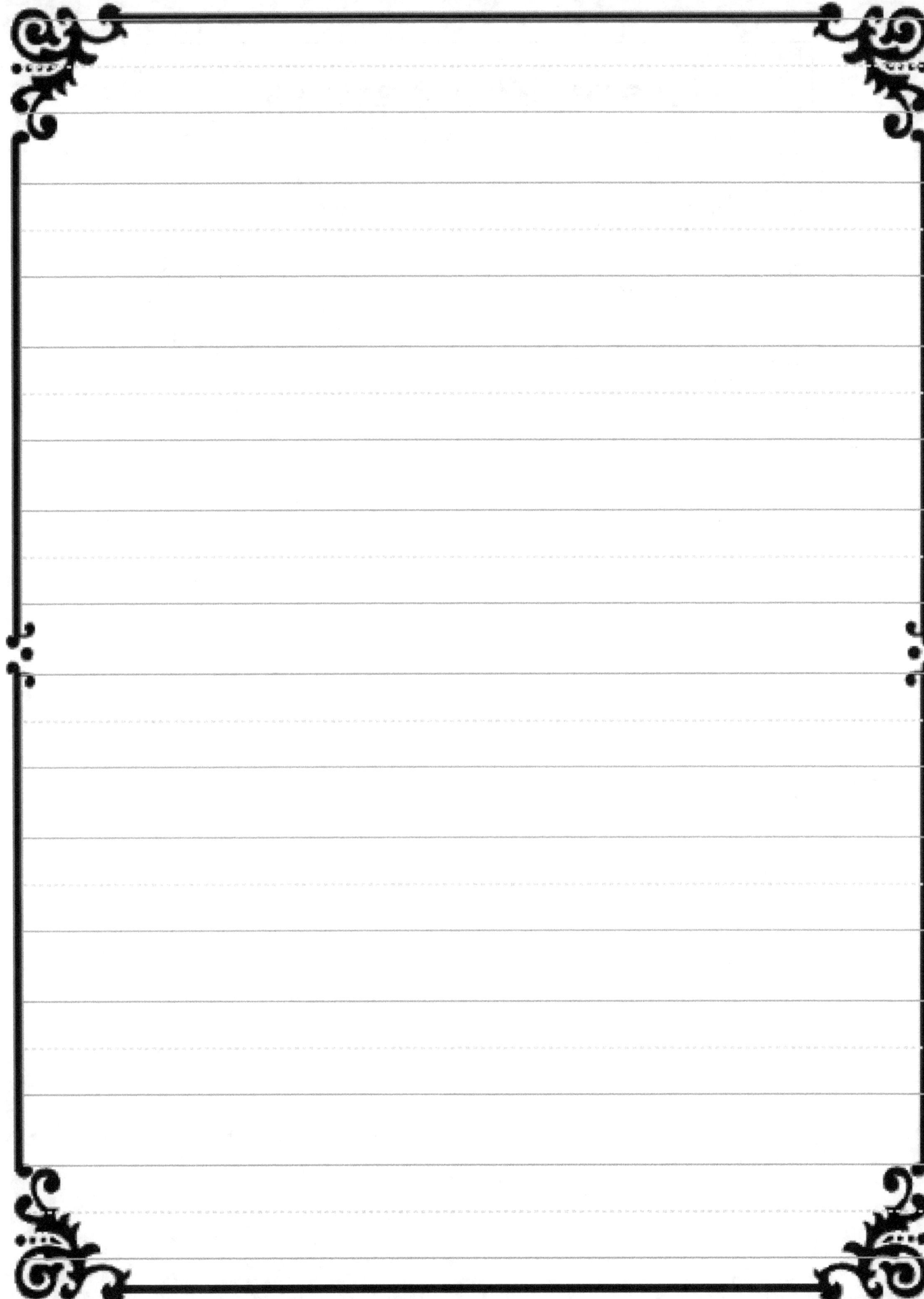

Trace The Letters

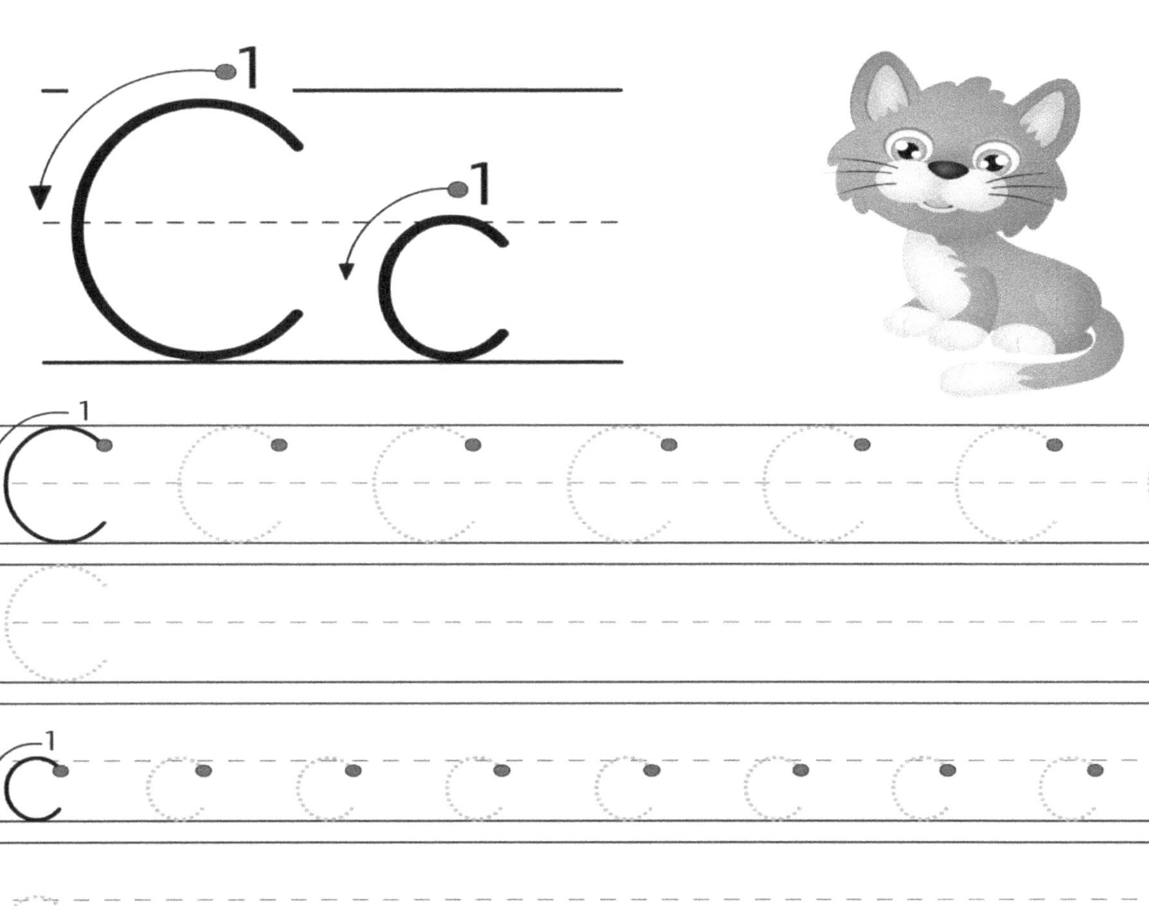

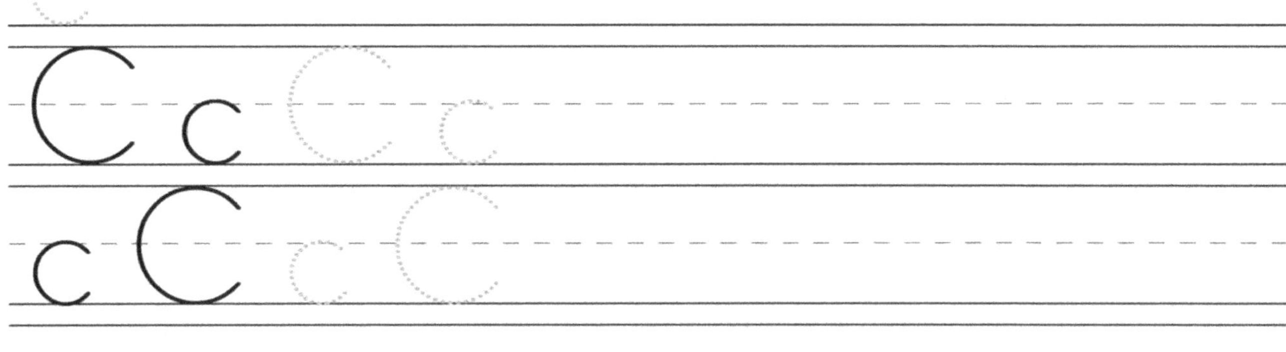

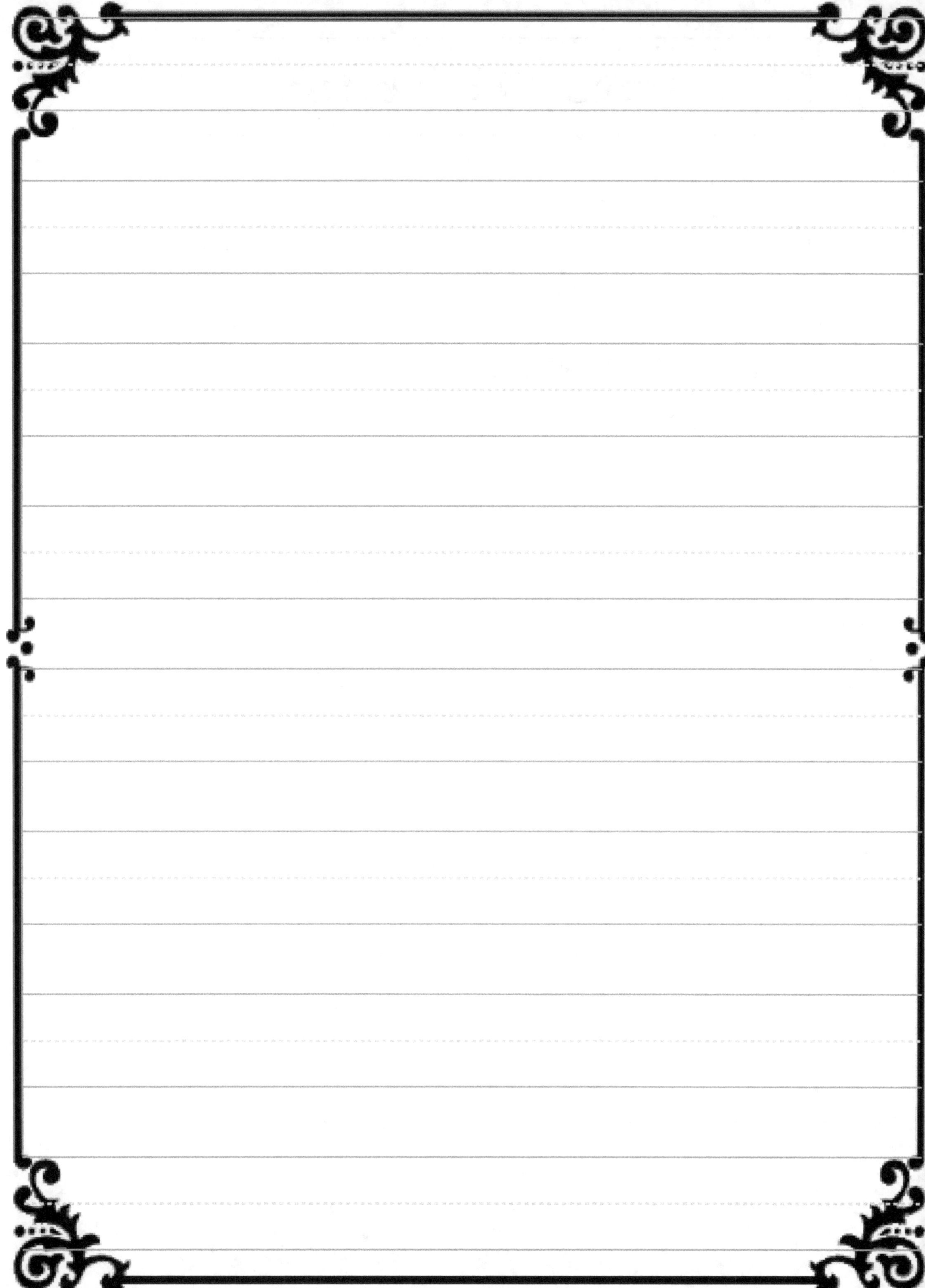

Trace The Letters

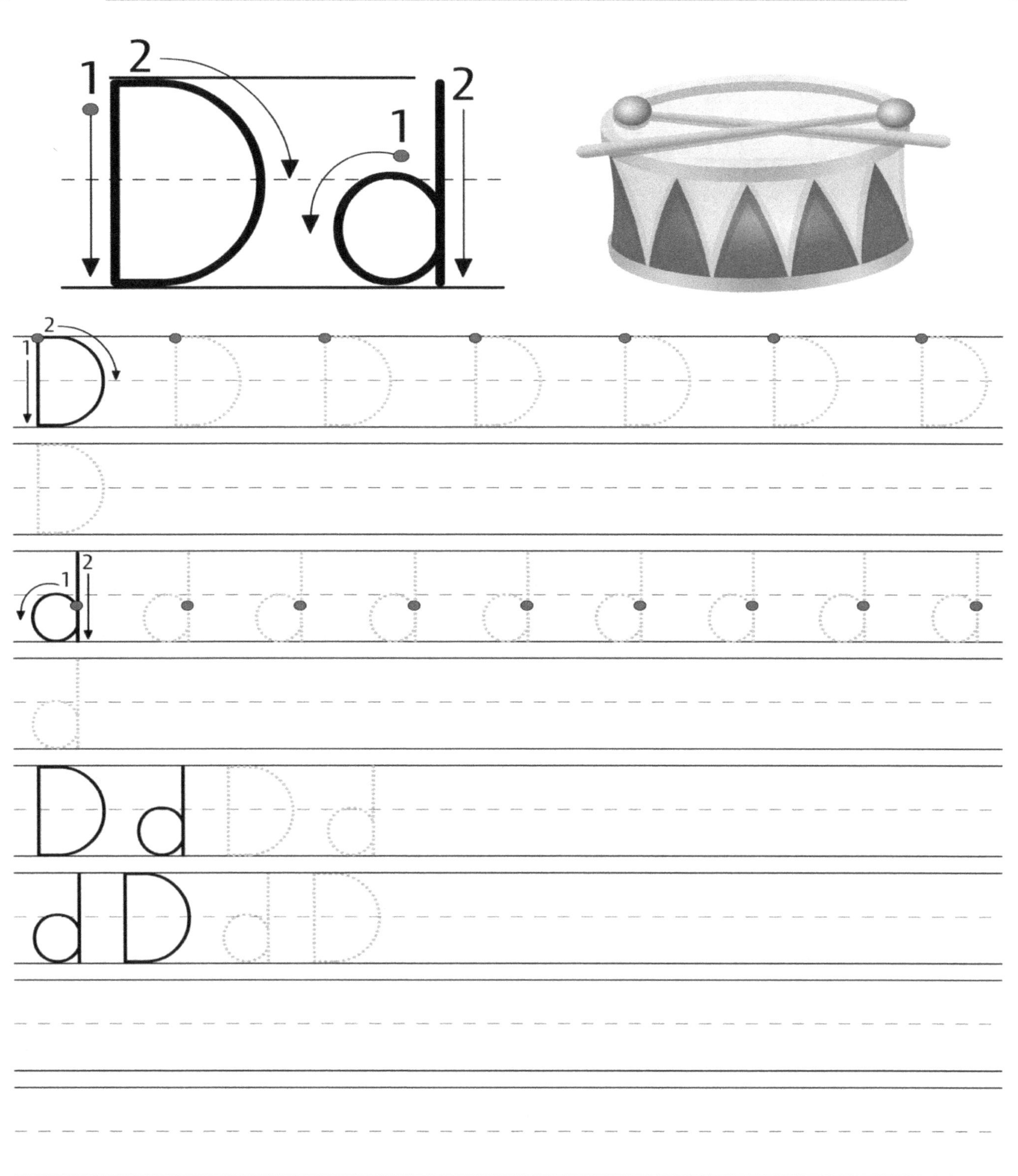

Trace The Letters

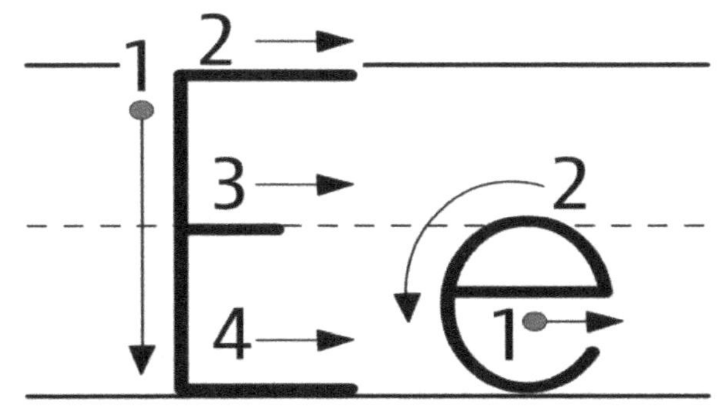

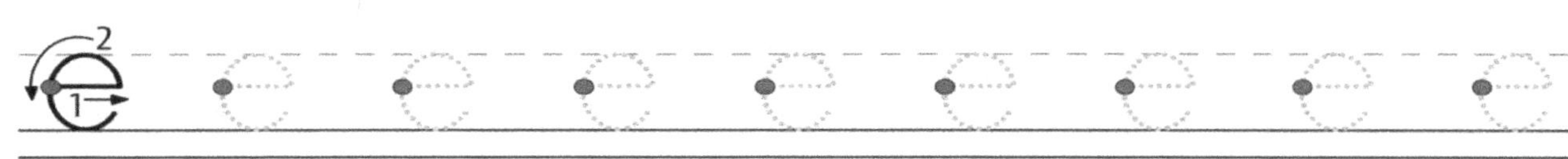

E e

e E

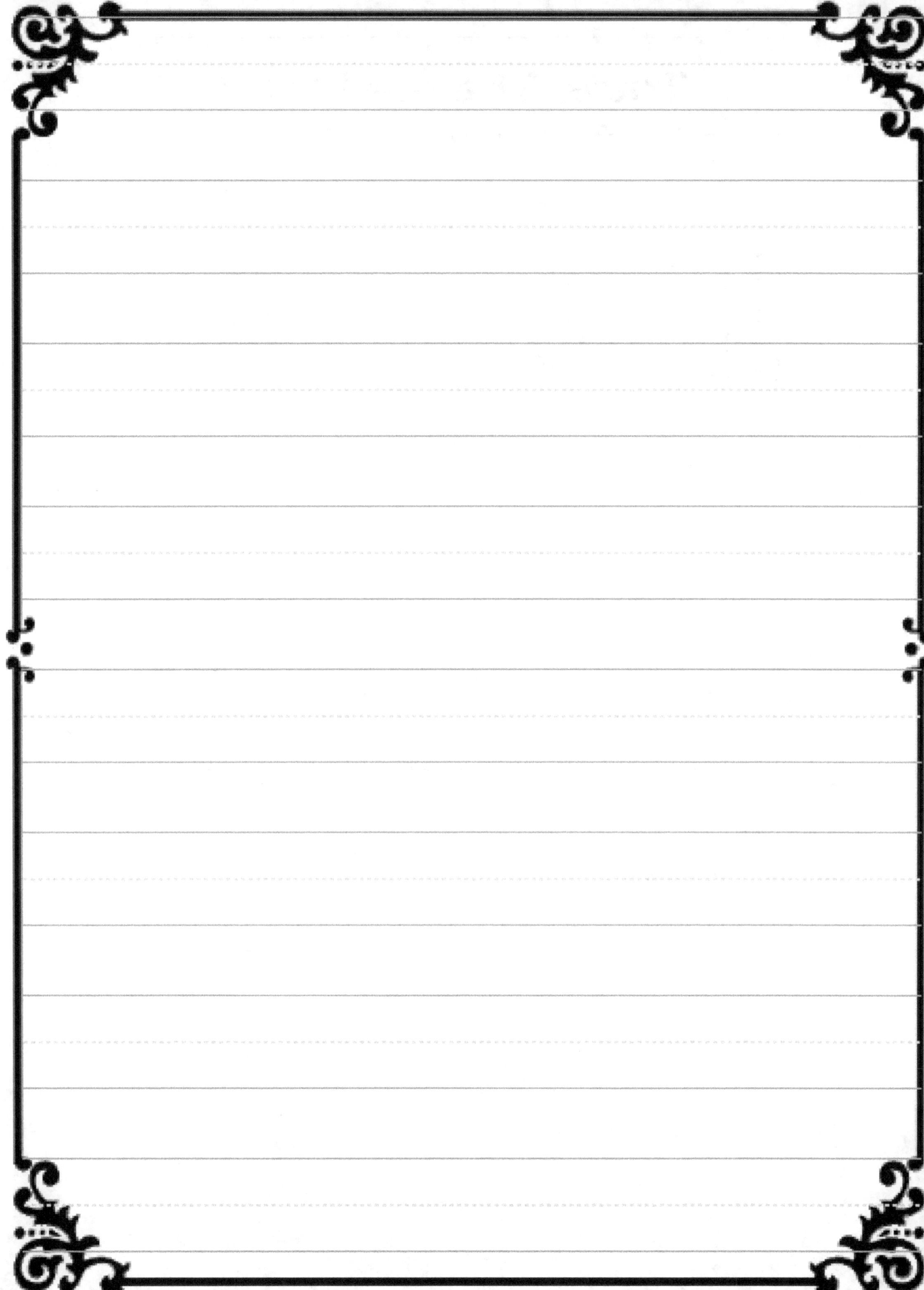

Trace The Letters

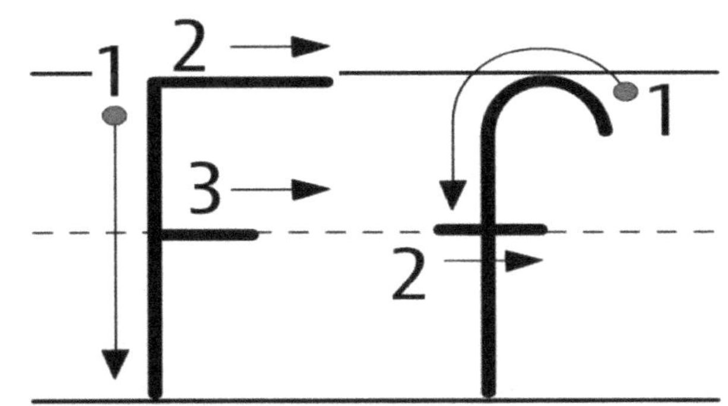

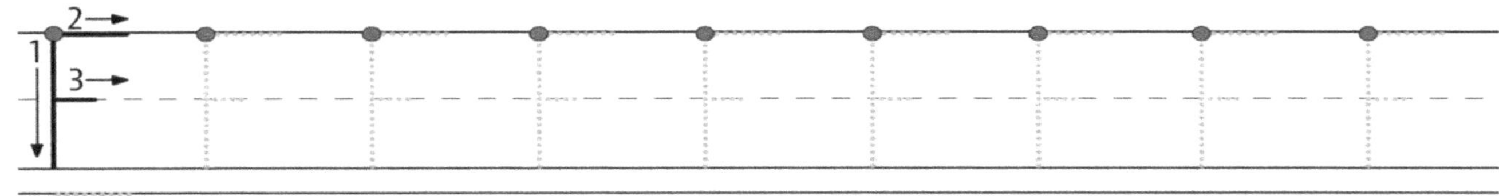

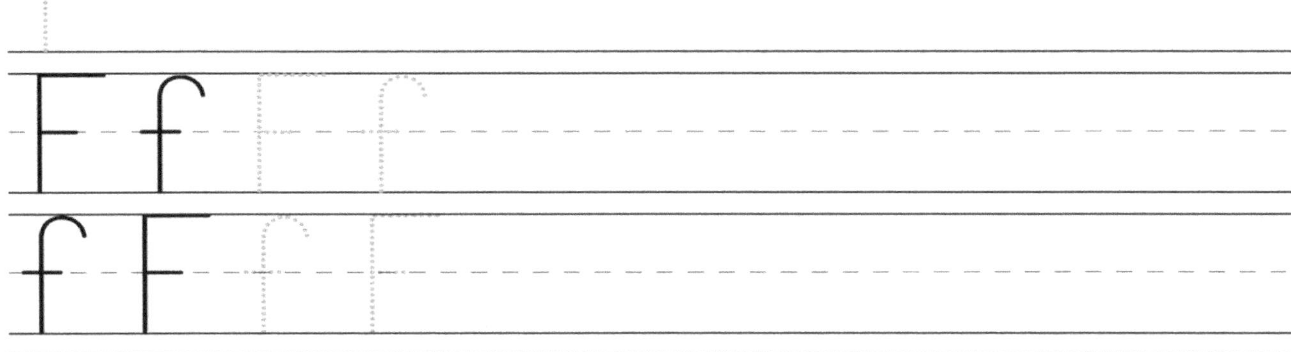

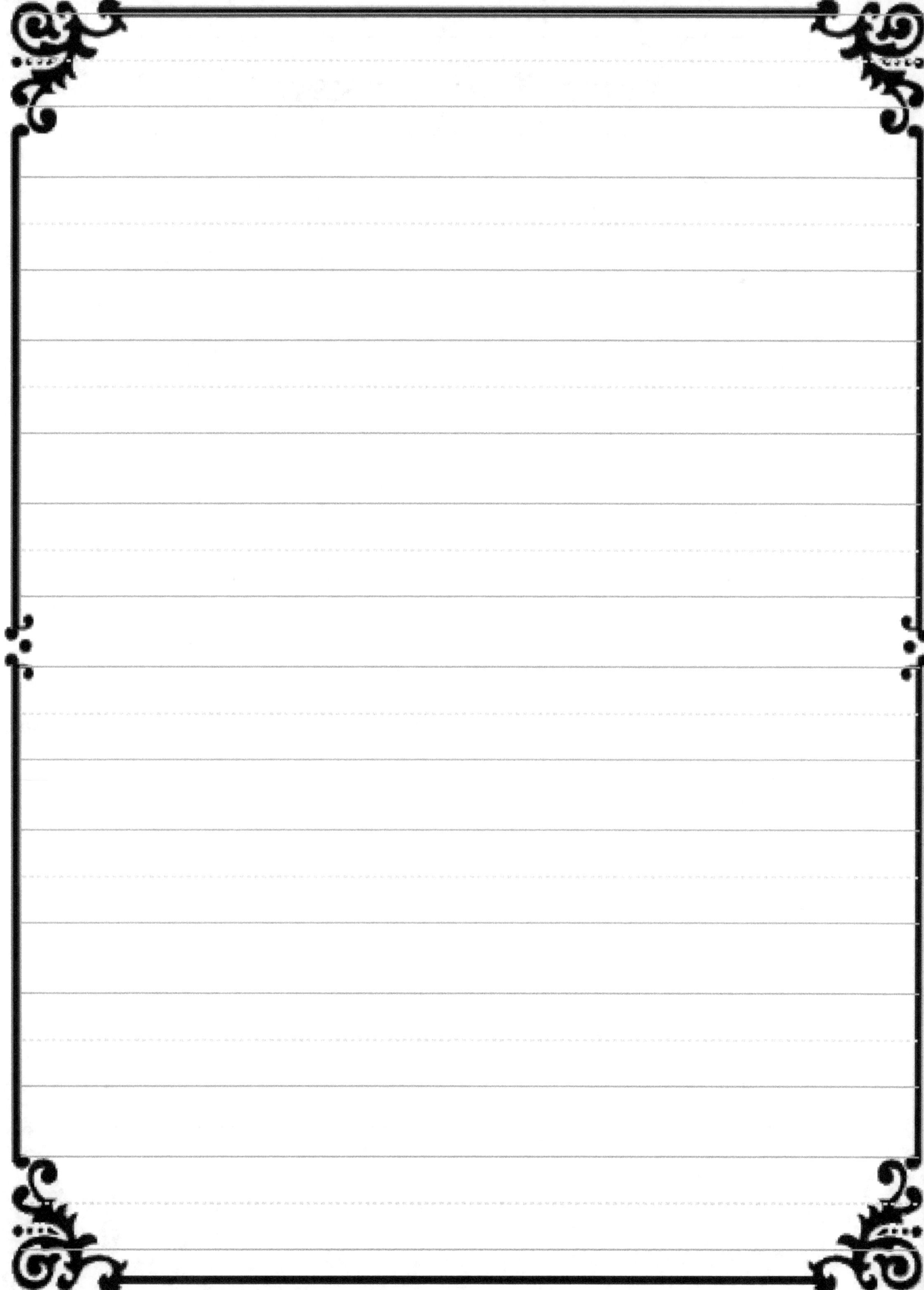

Trace The Letters

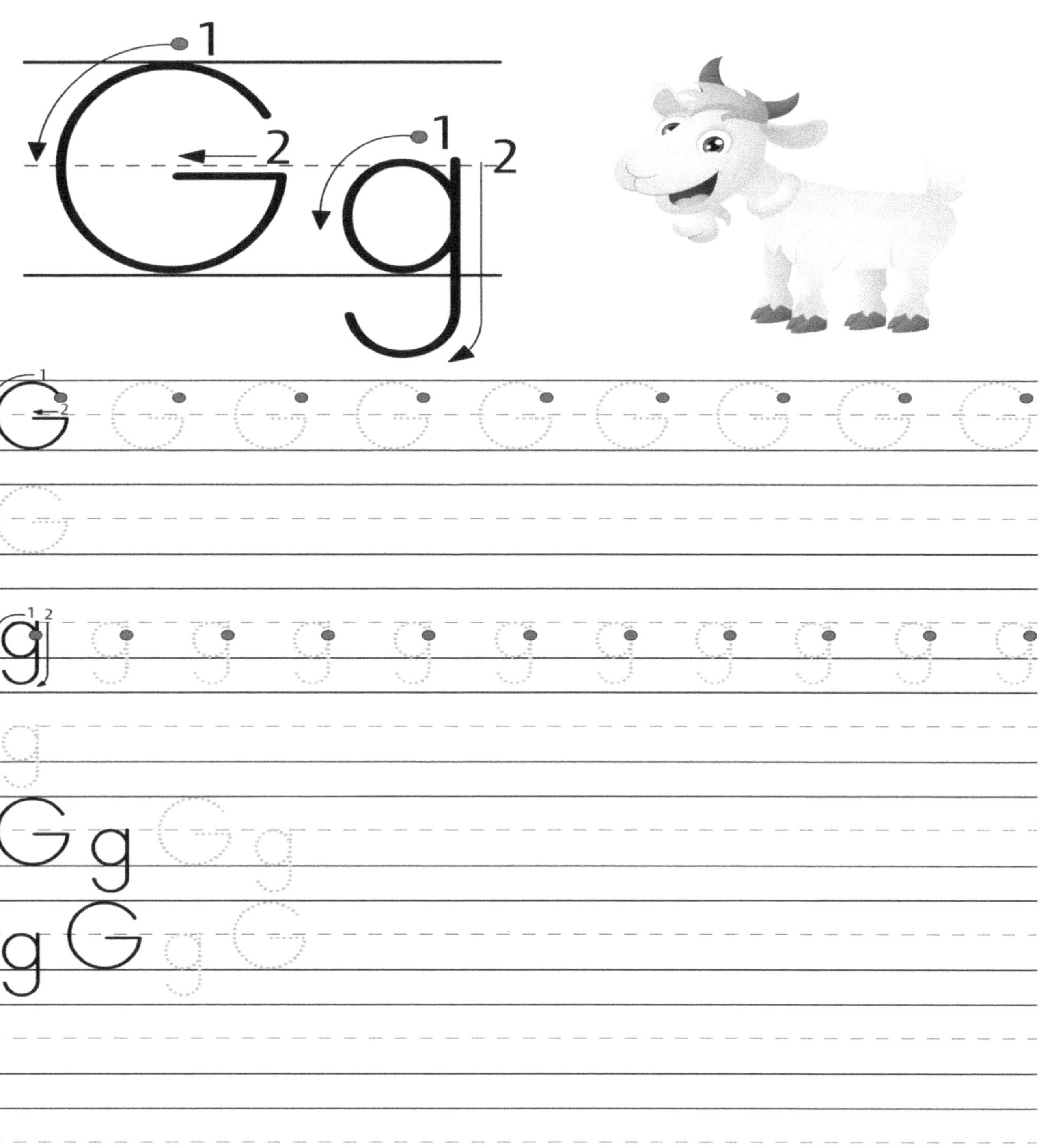

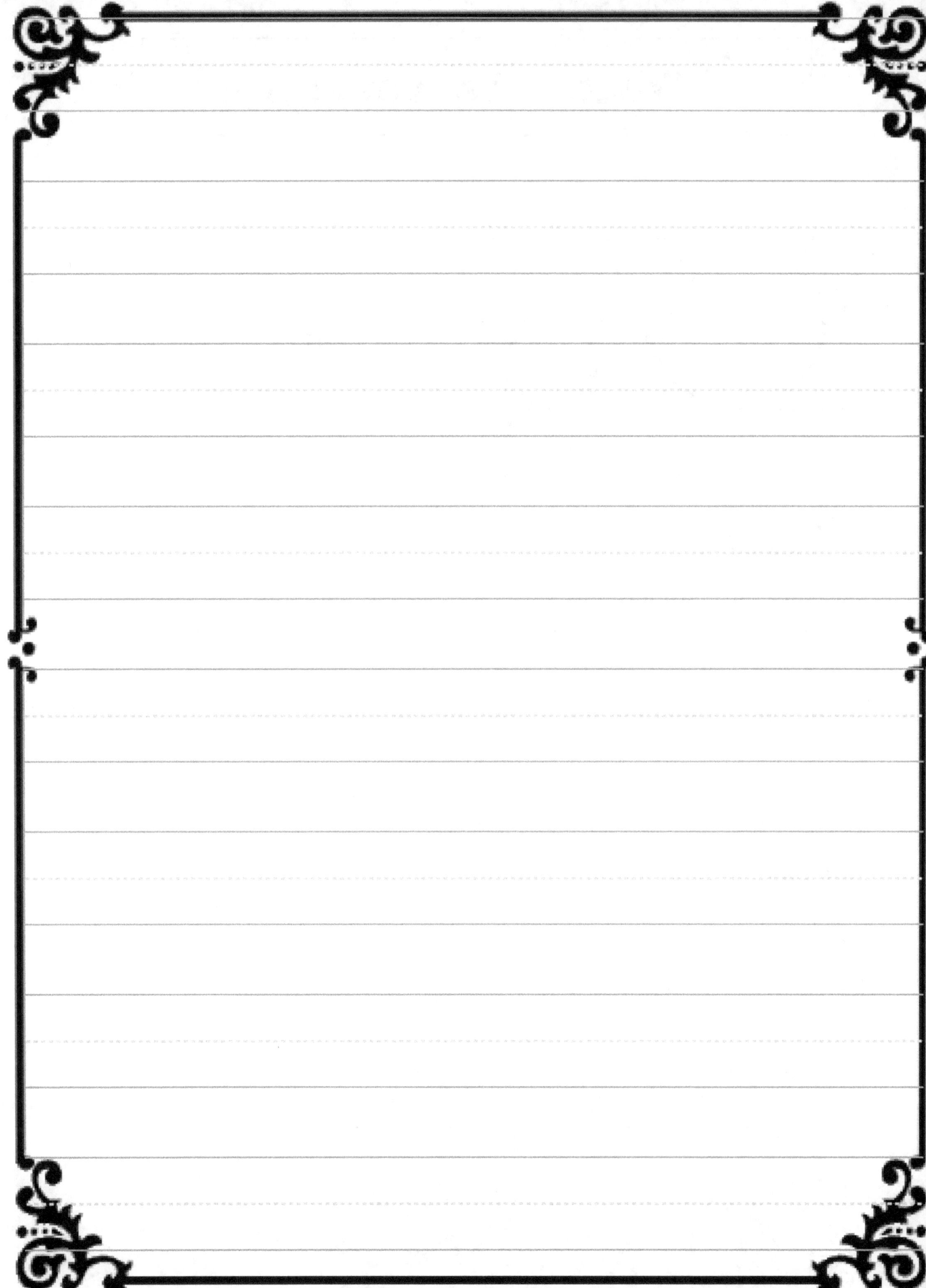

Trace The Letters

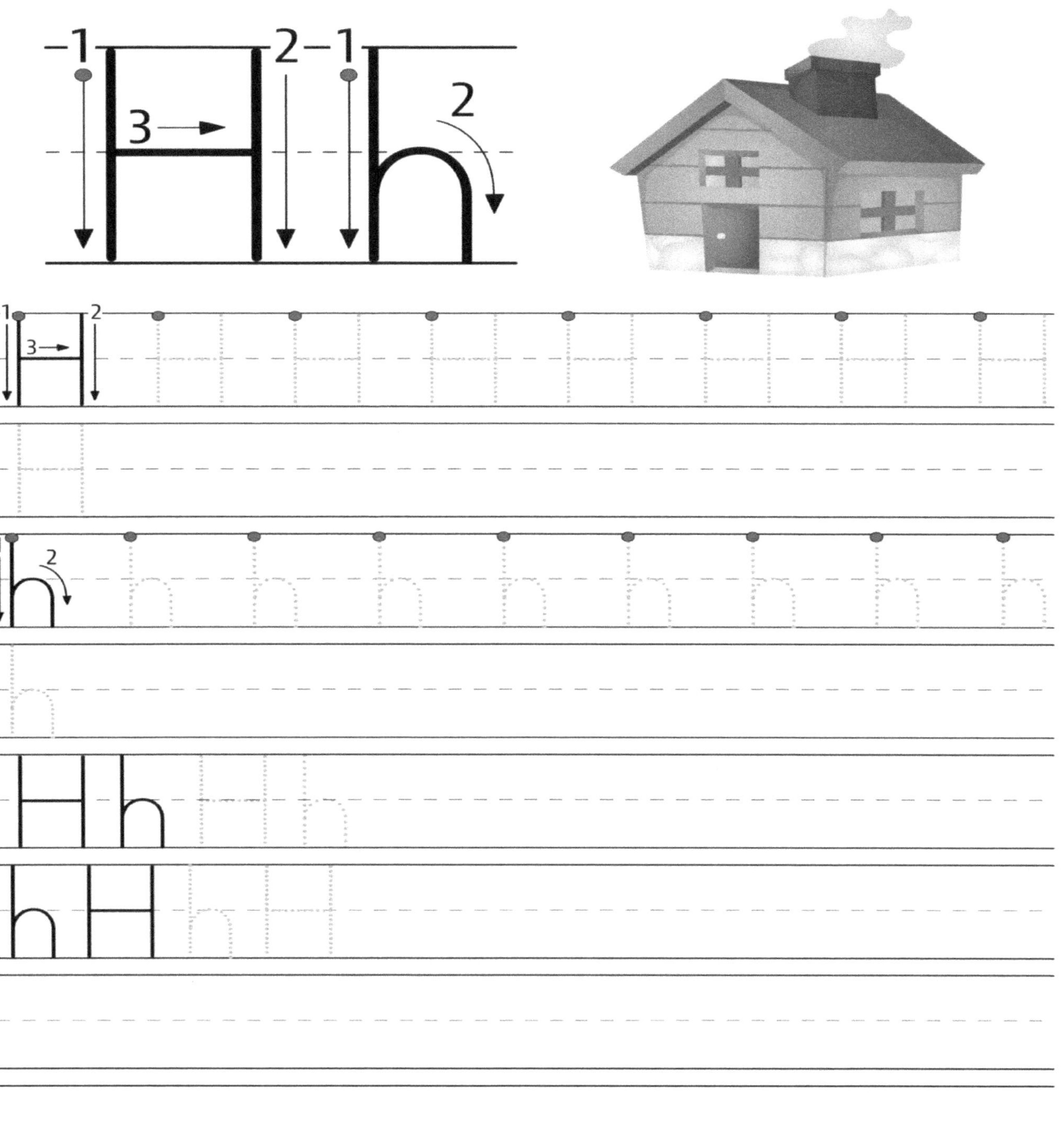

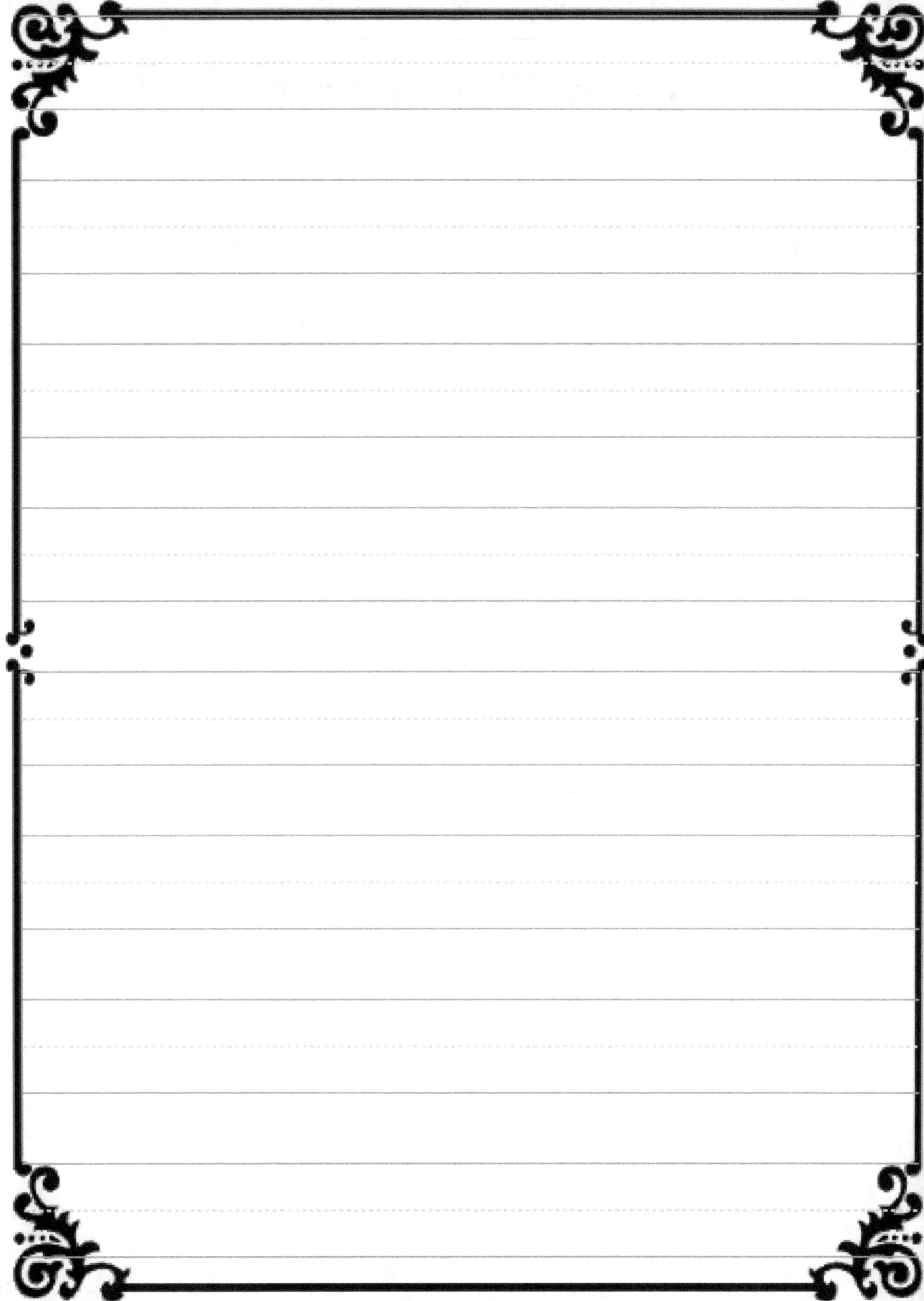

Trace The Letters

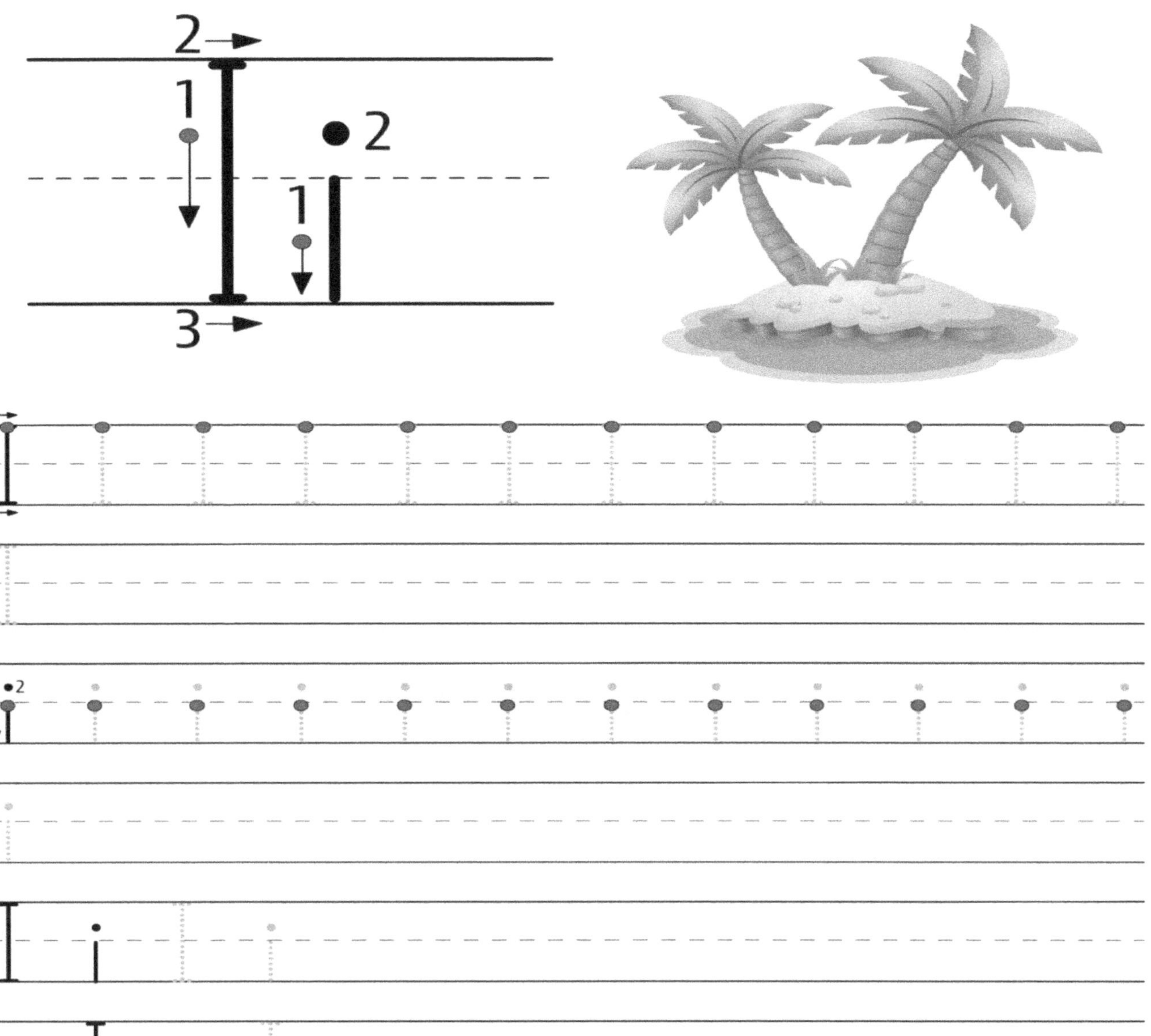

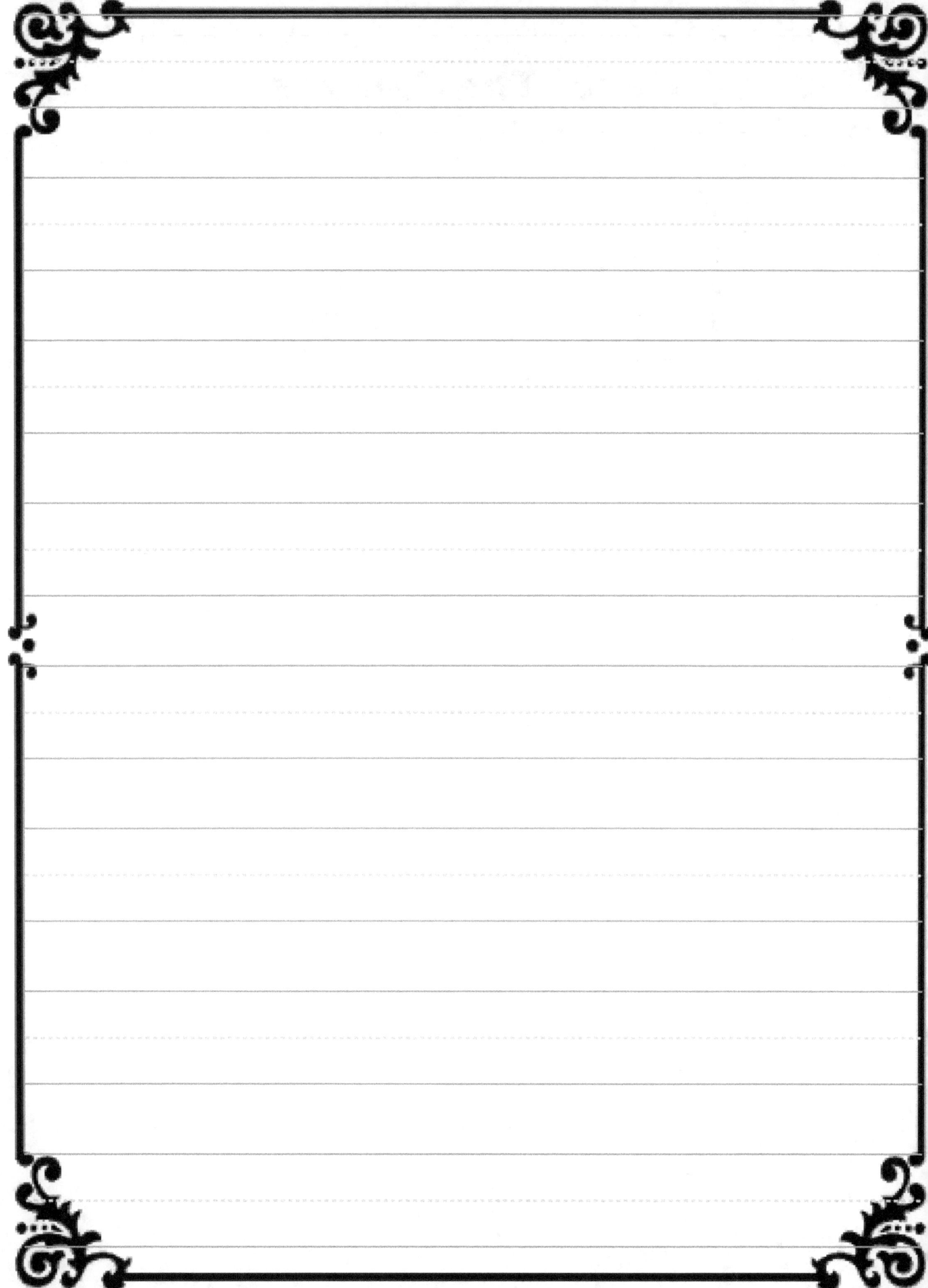

Trace The Letters

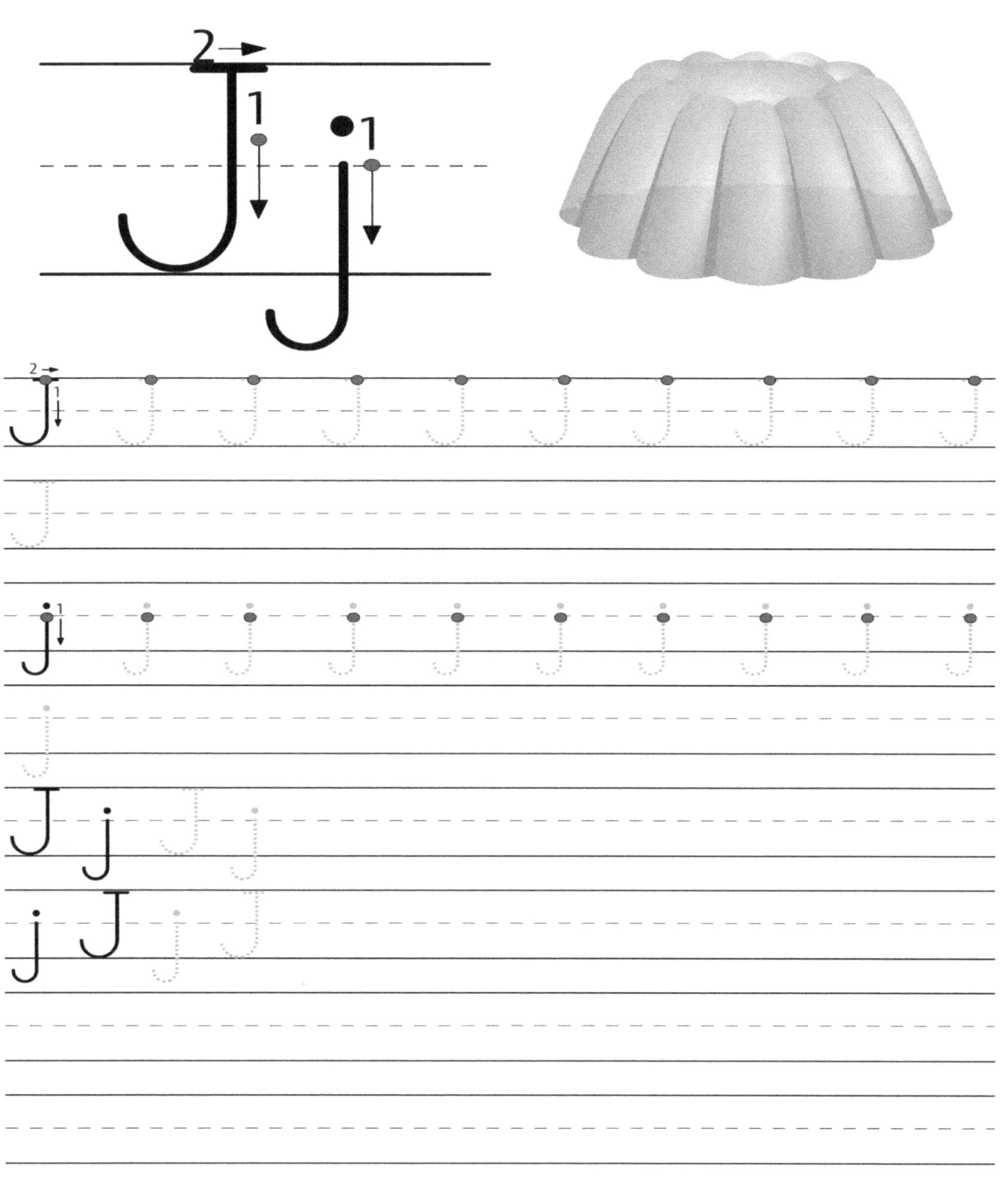

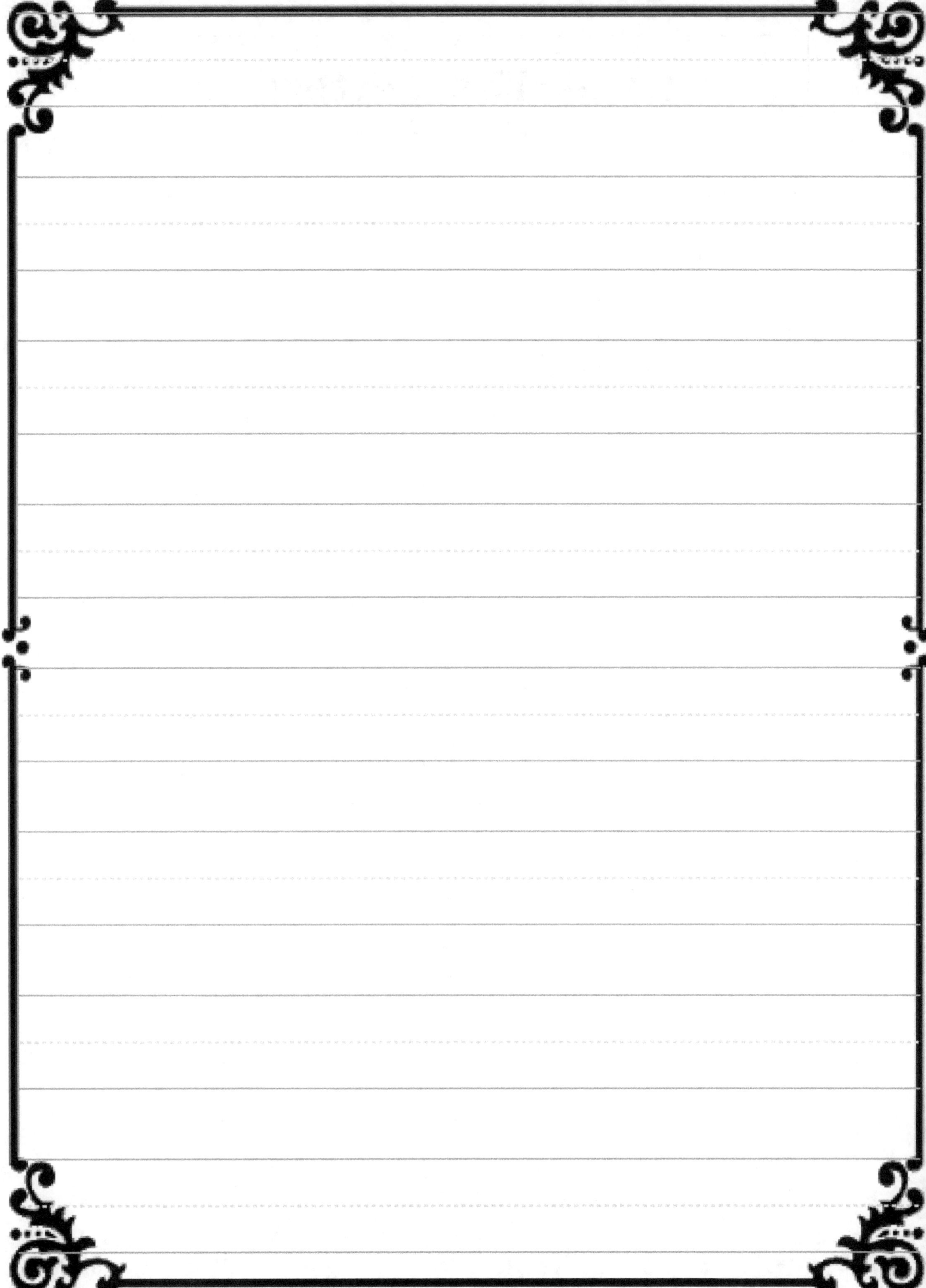

Trace The Letters

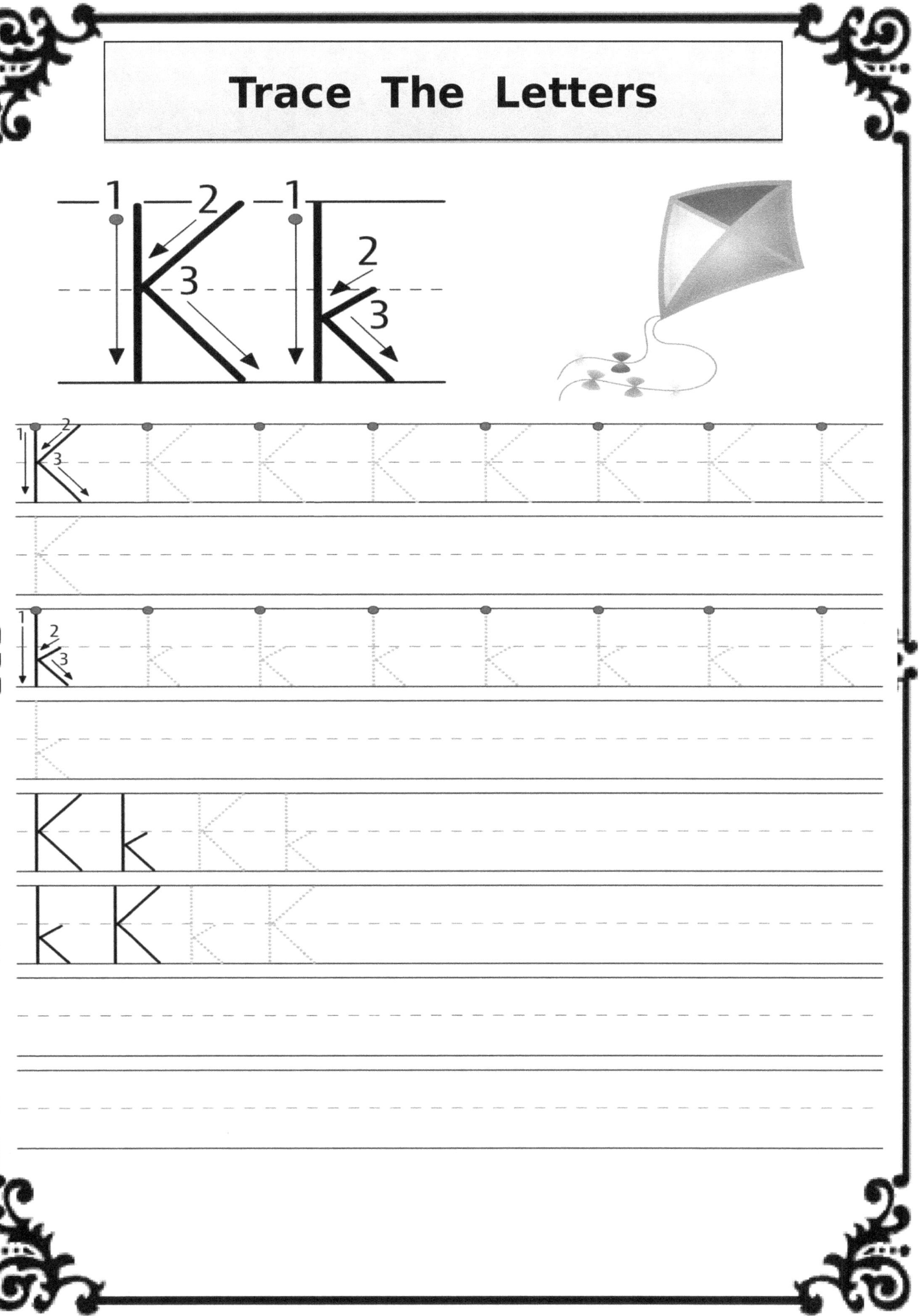

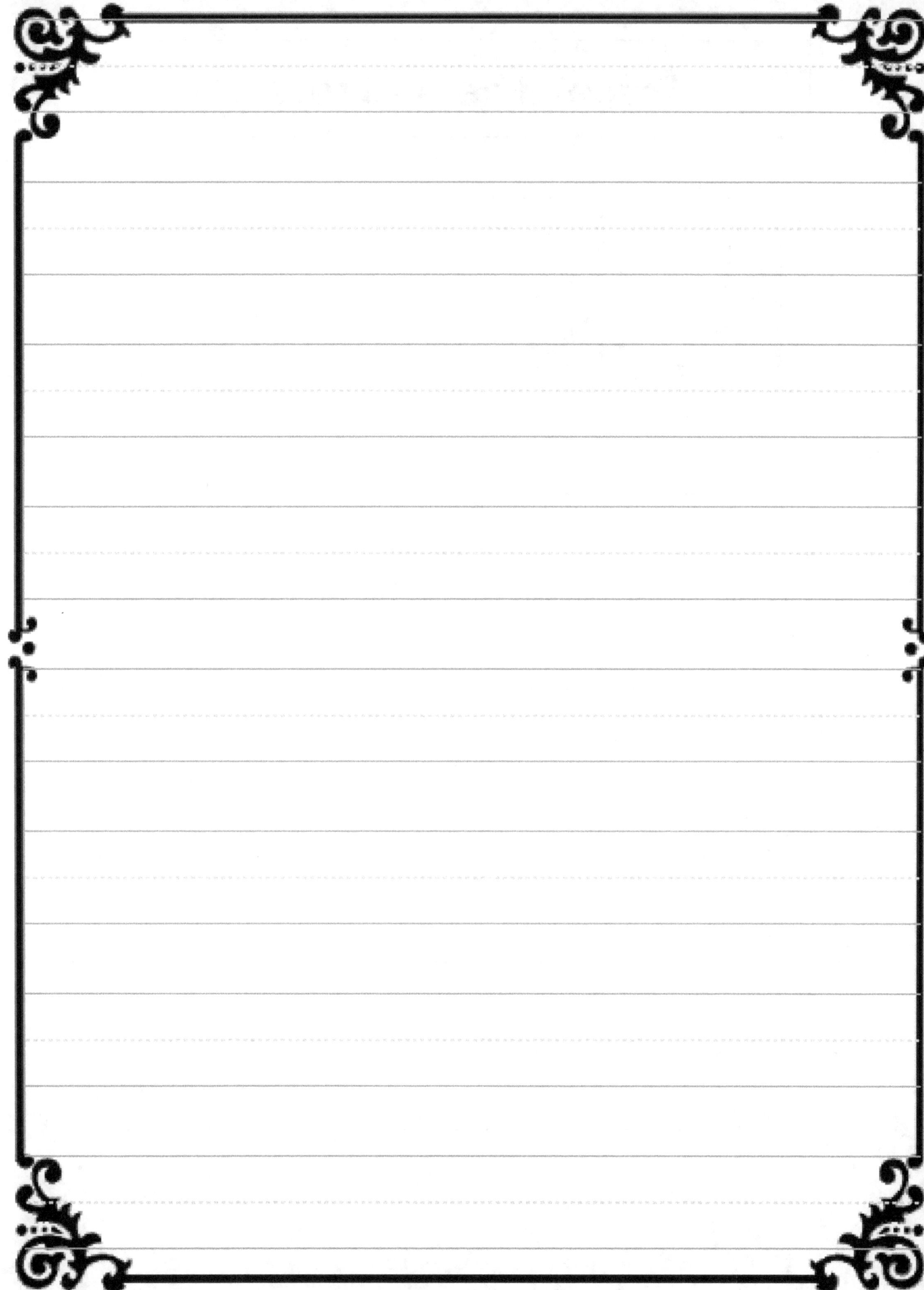

Trace The Letters

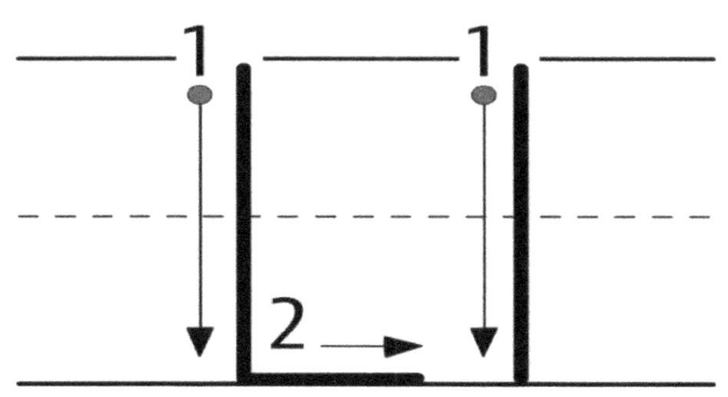

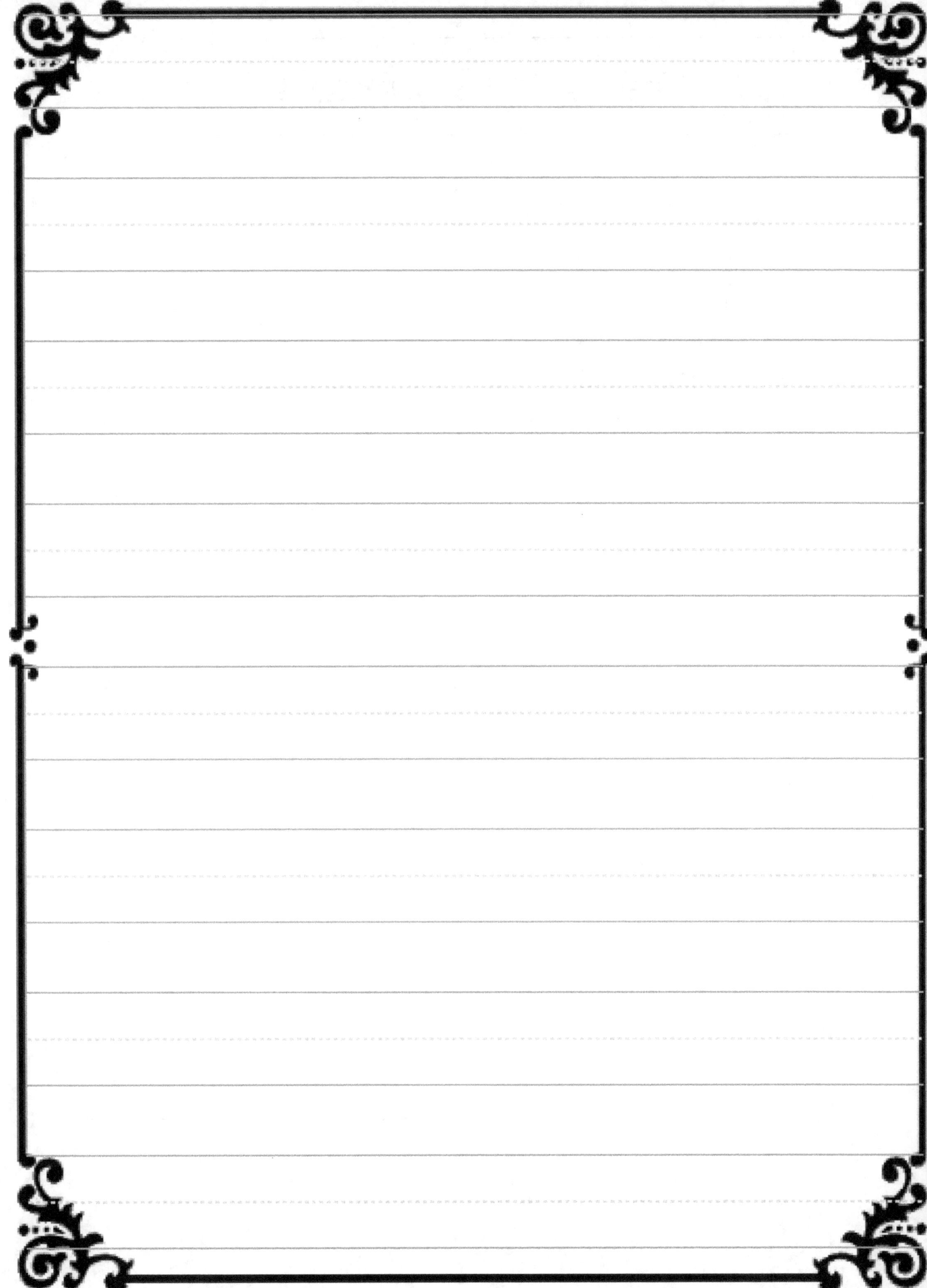

Trace The Letters

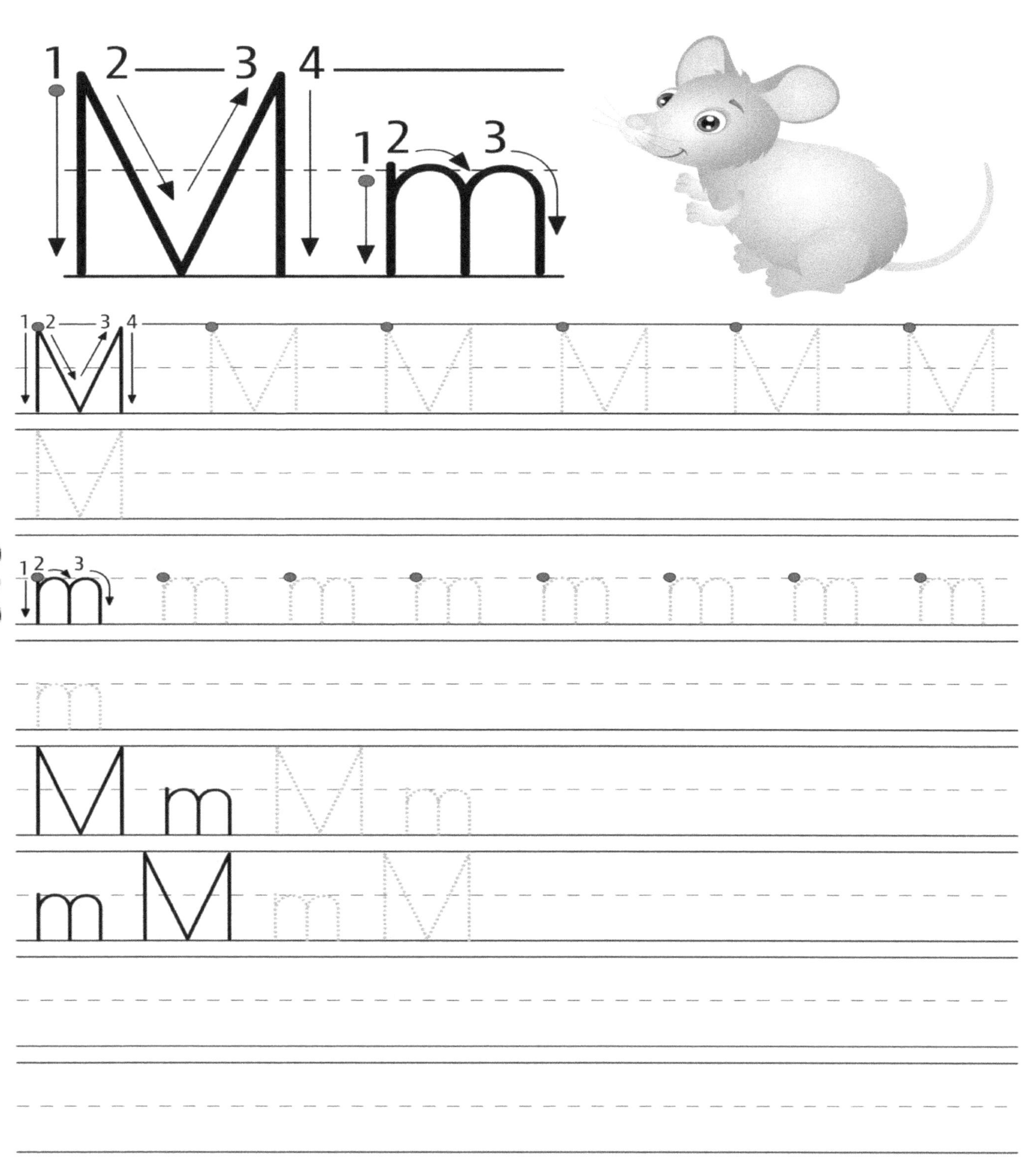

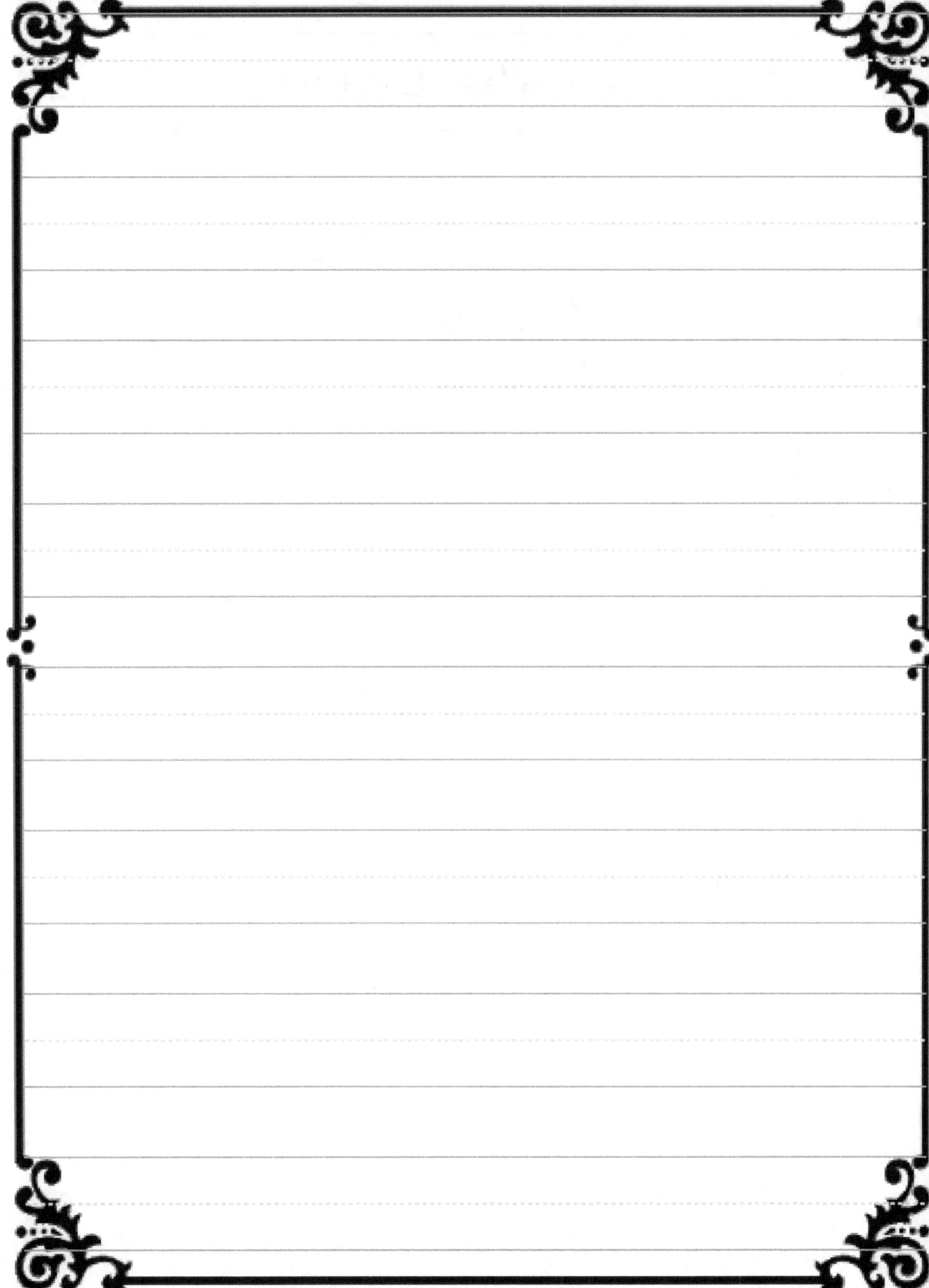

Trace The Letters

1 2 3 N 1 2 n

N N N N N N N

N

n n n n n n n n n n

n

N n N n

n N n N

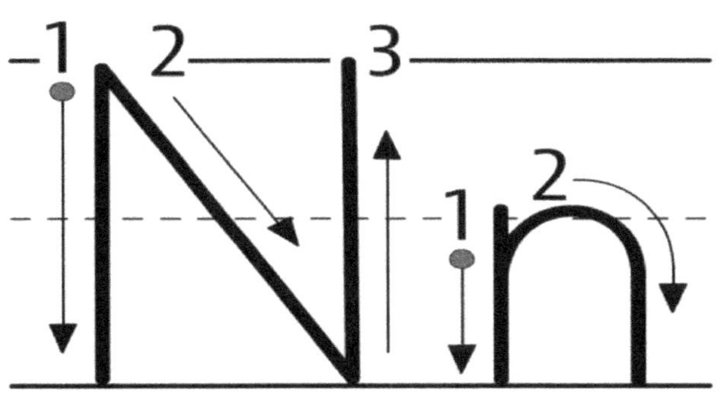

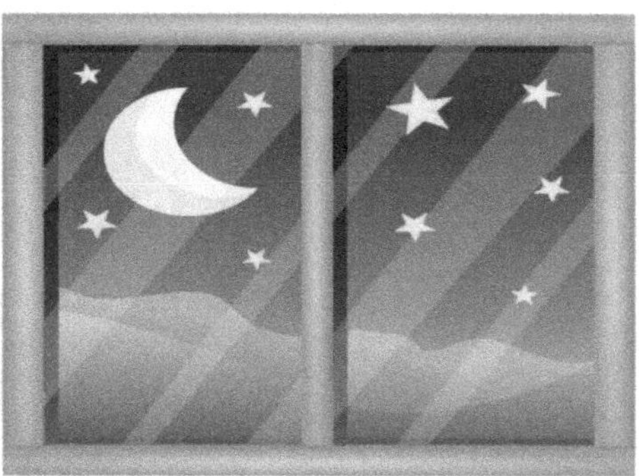

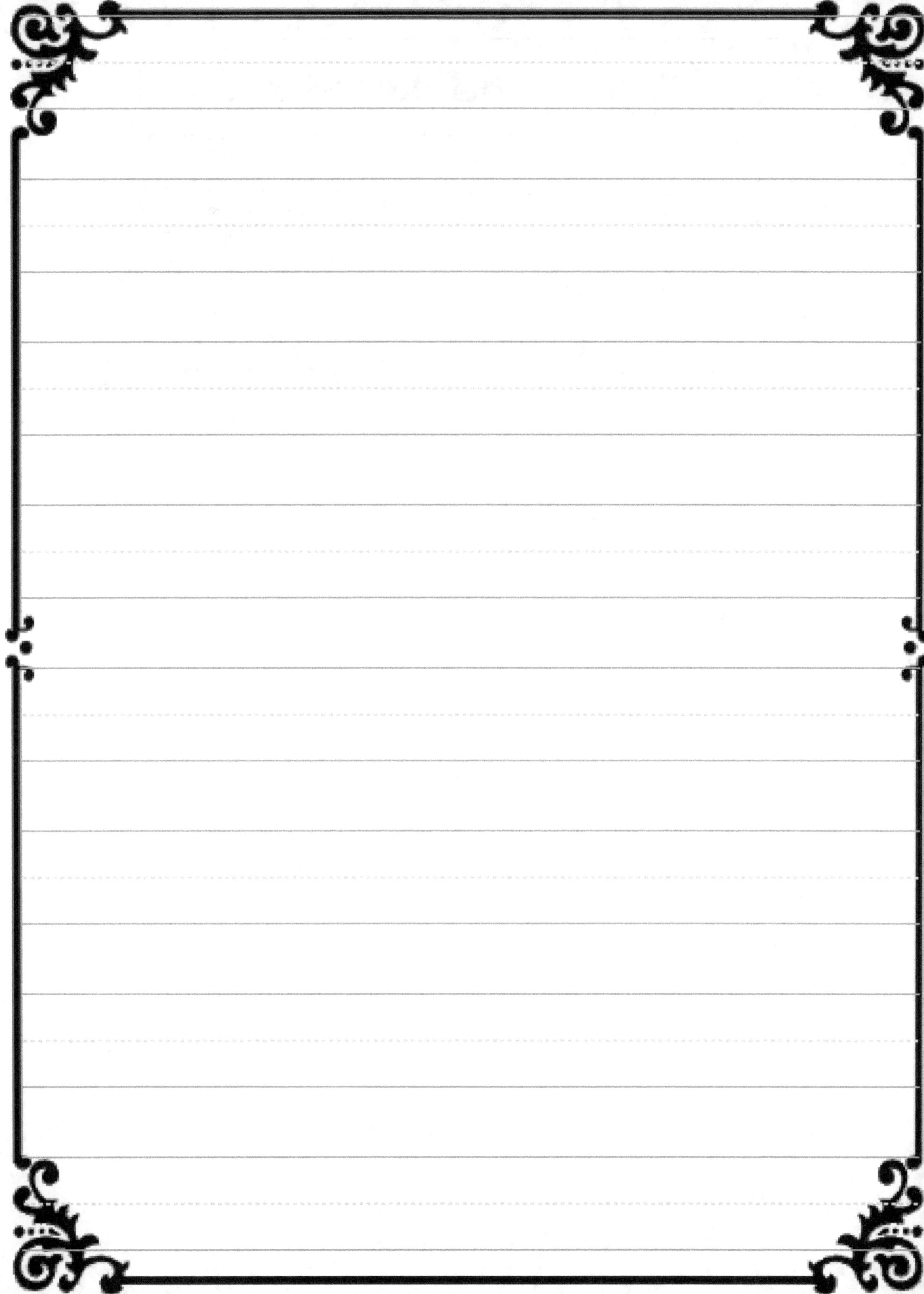

Trace The Letters

Trace The Letters

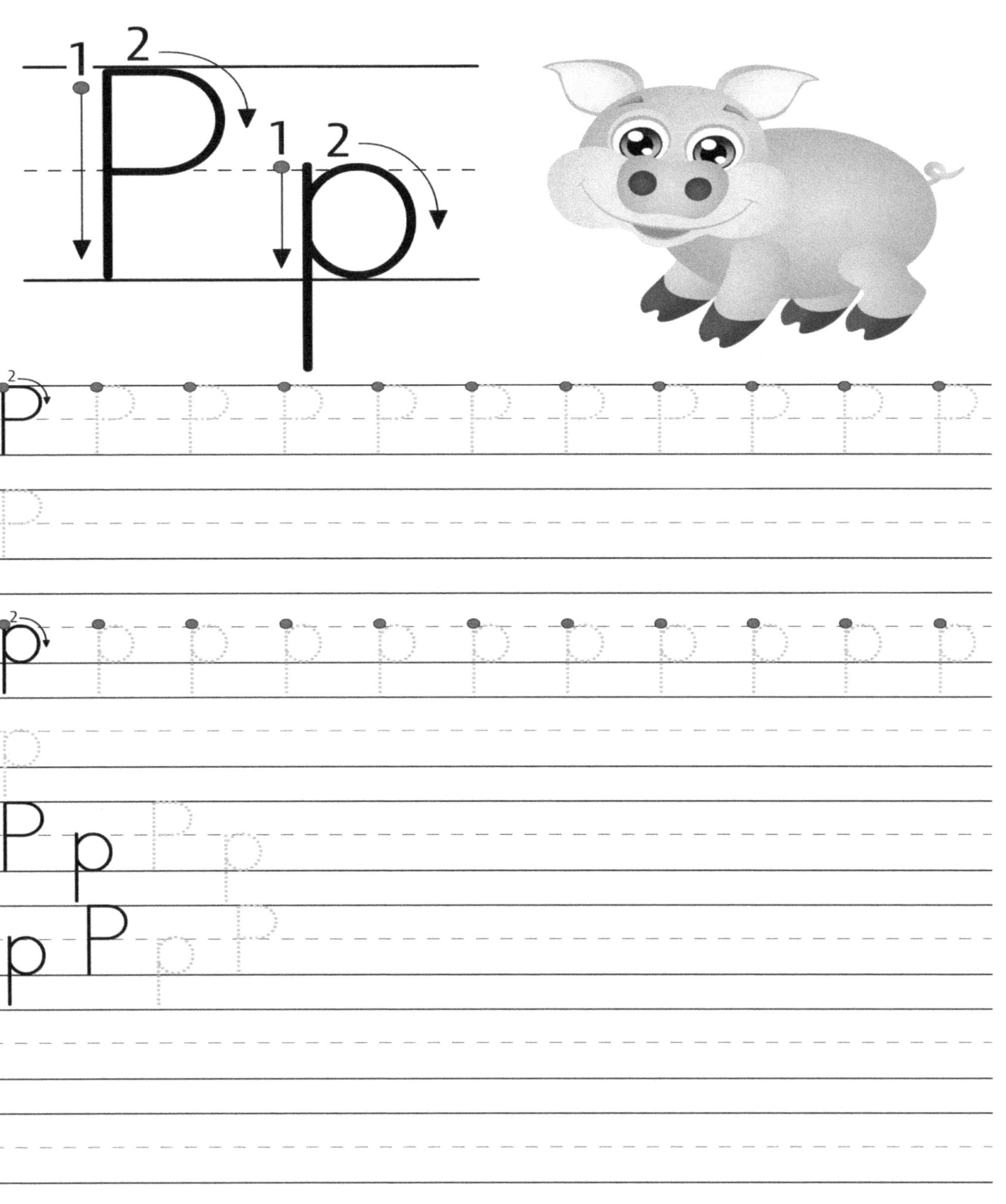

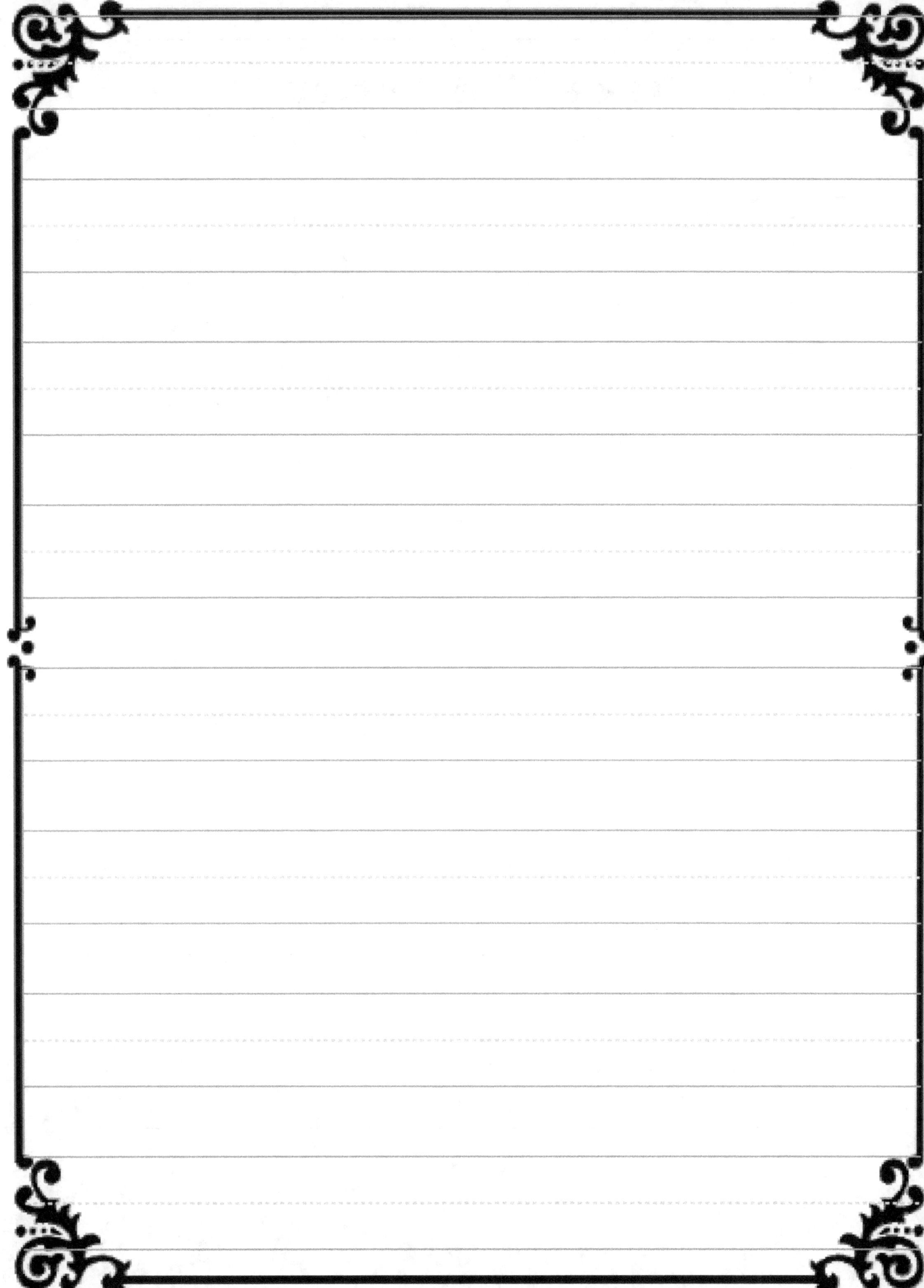

Trace The Letters

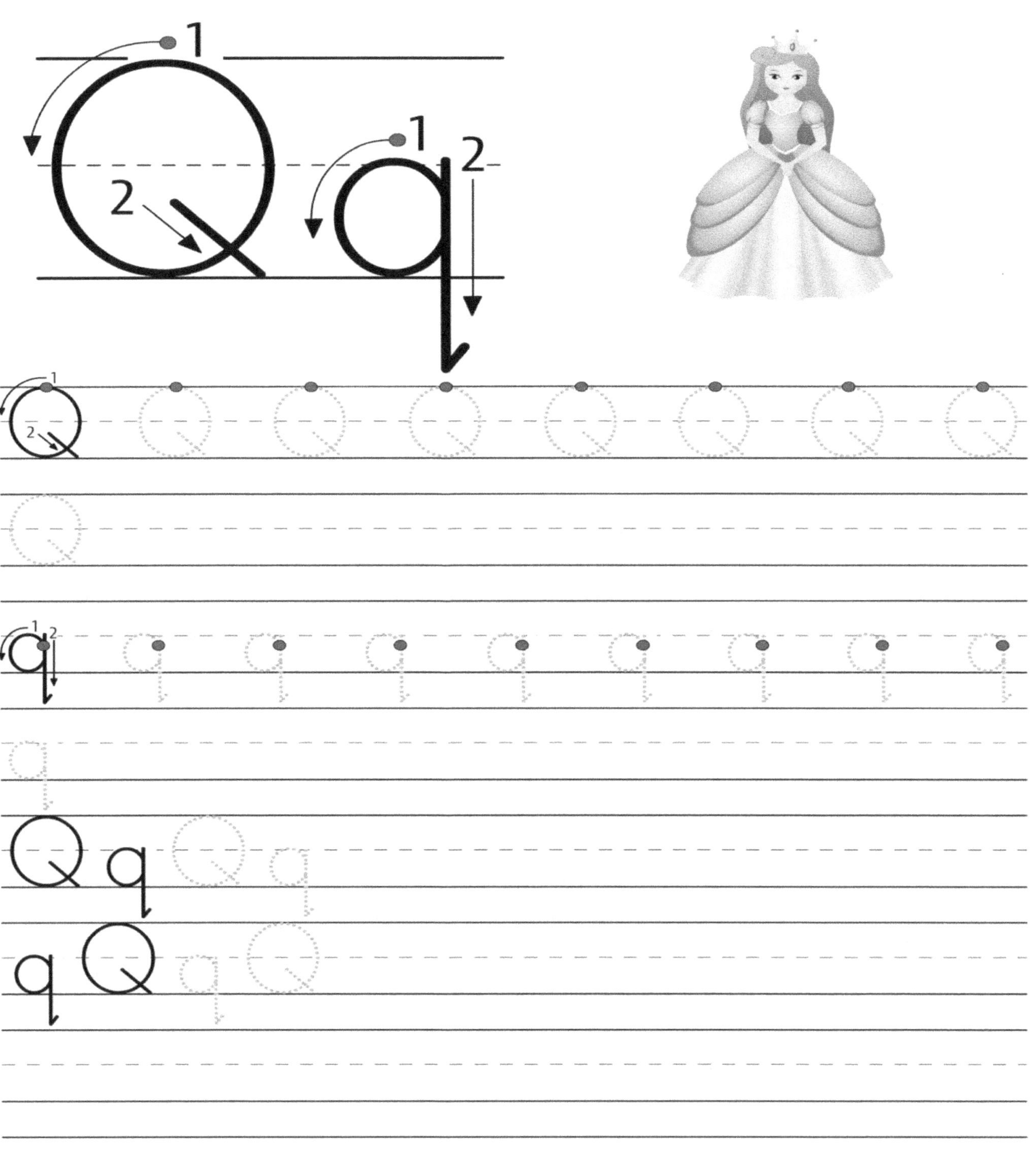

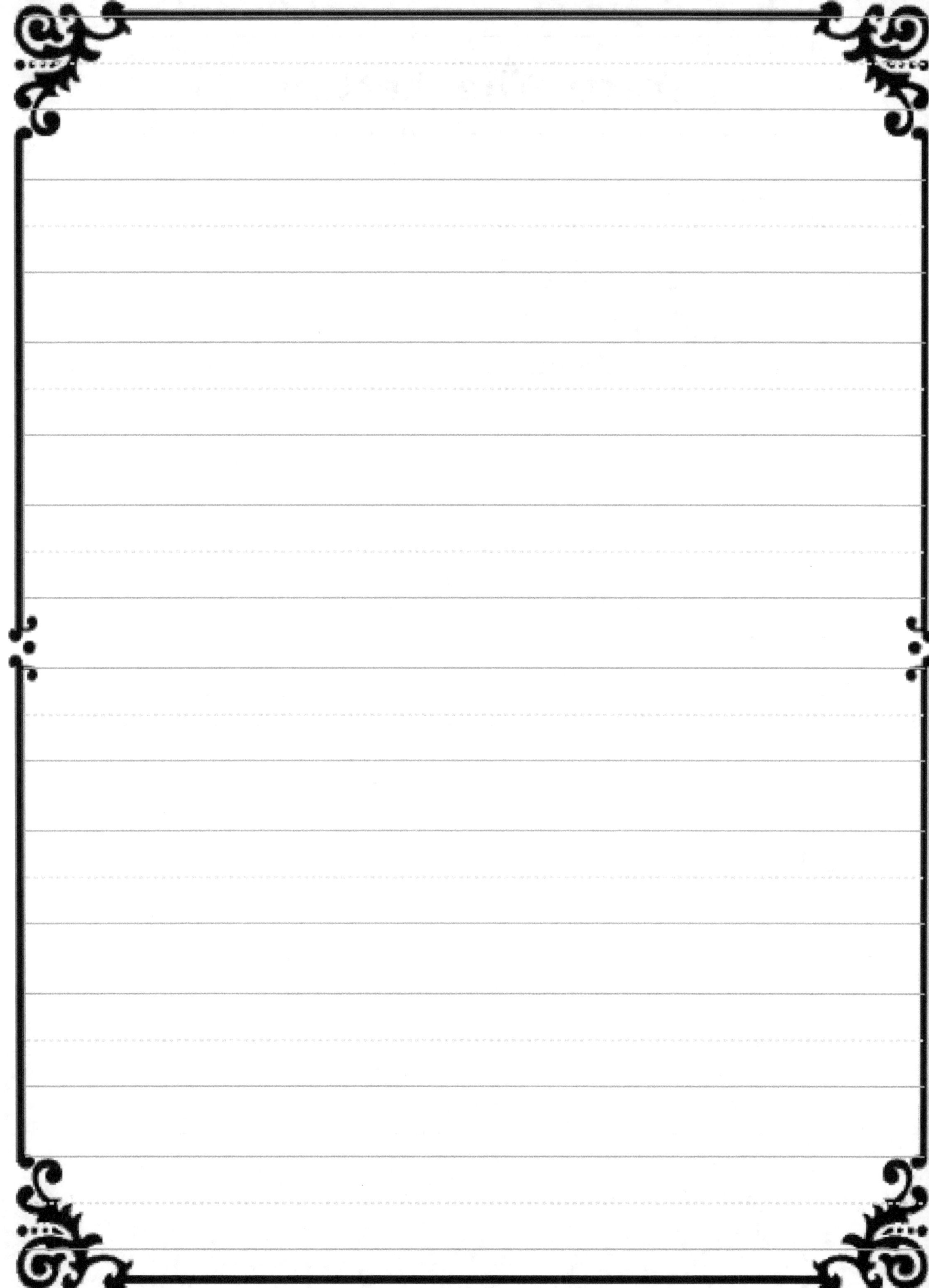

Trace The Letters

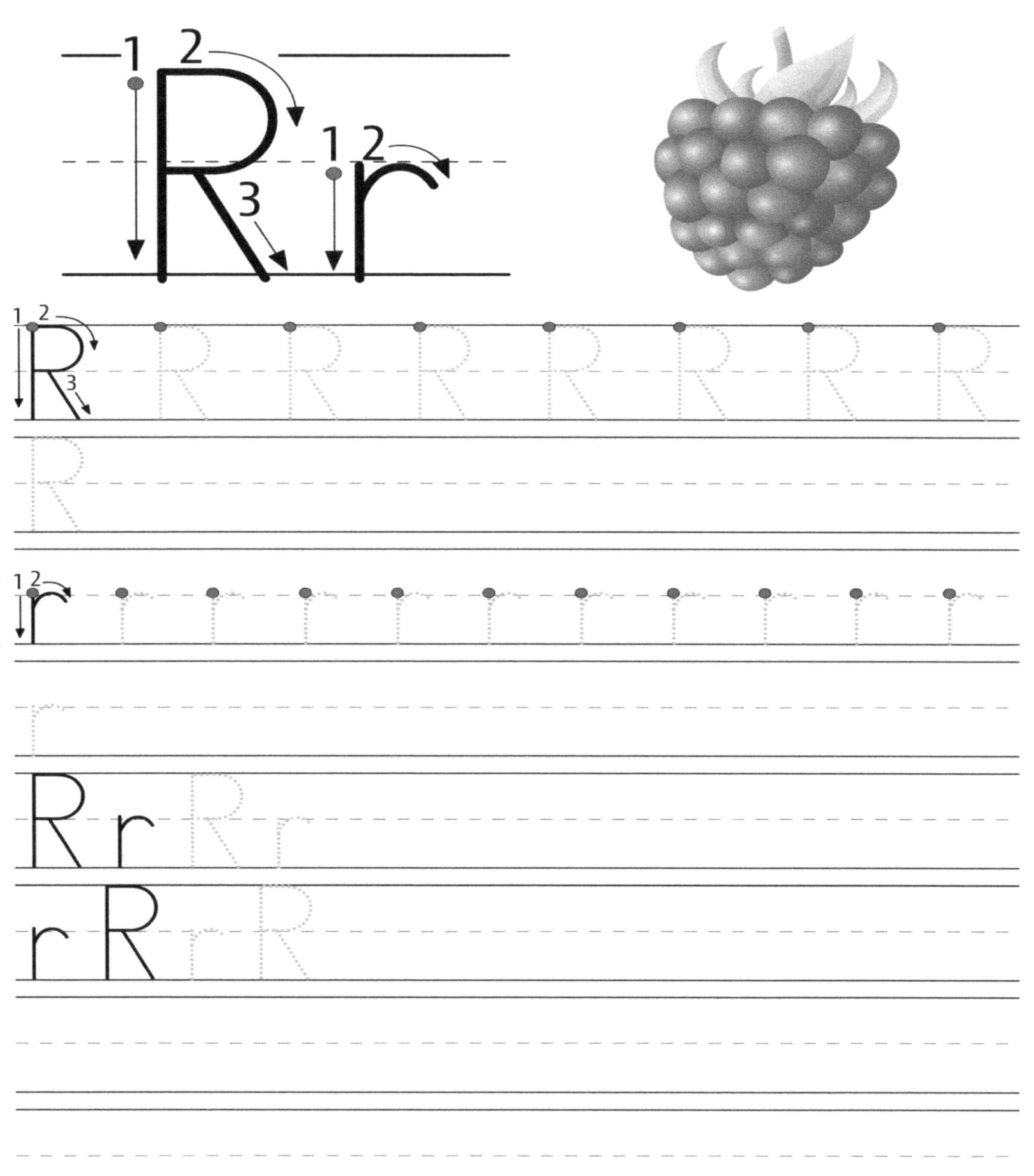

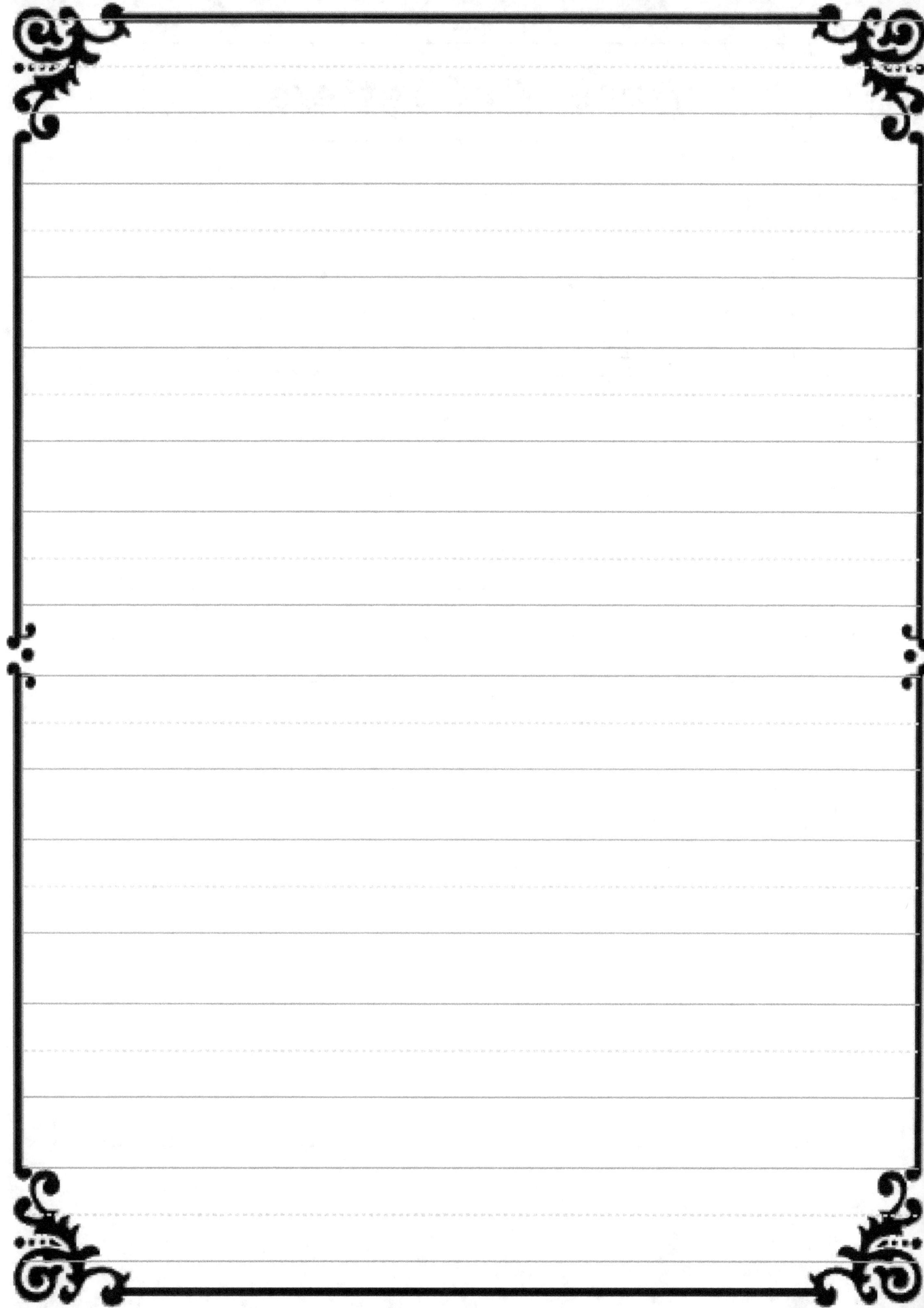

Trace The Letters

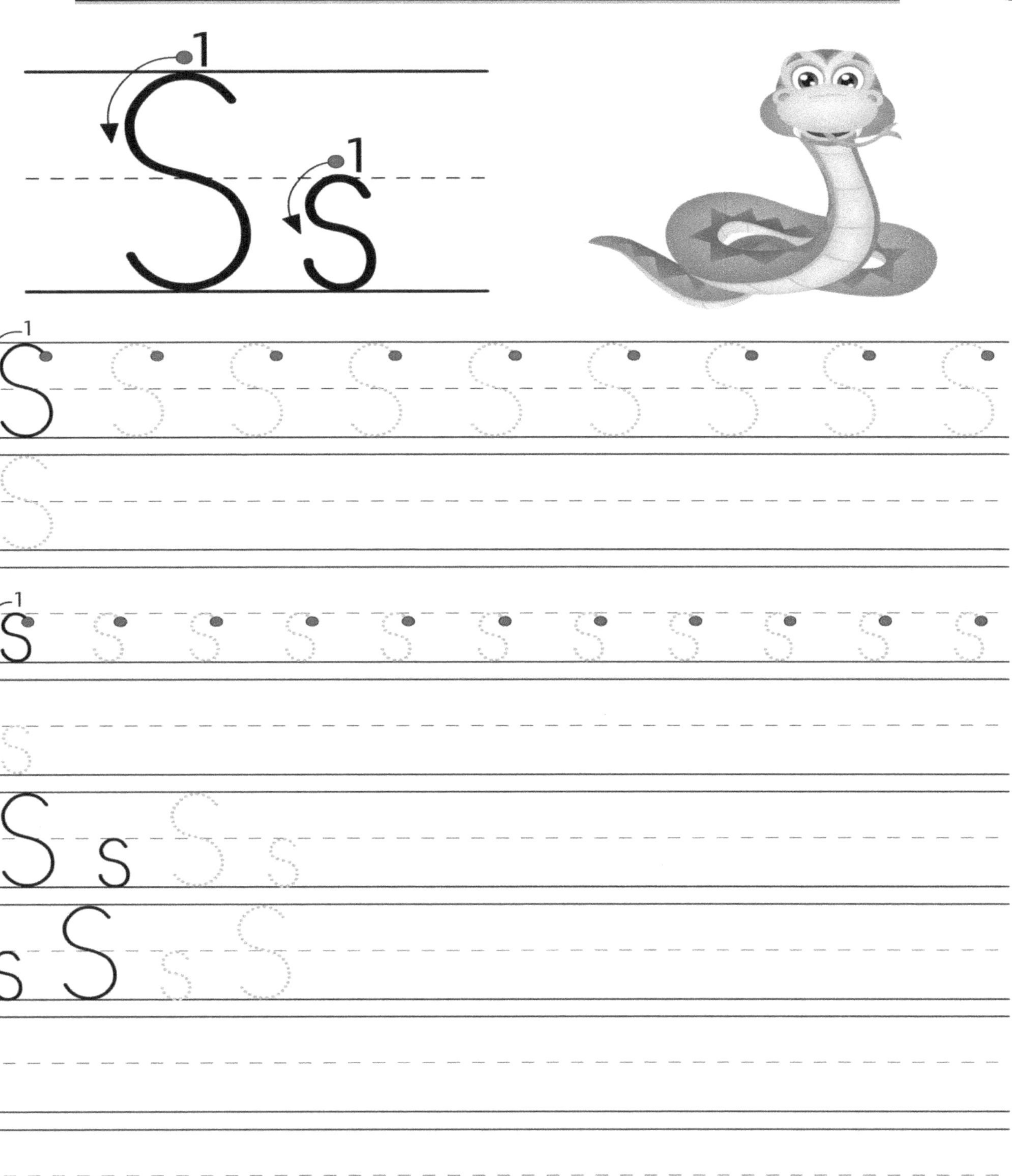

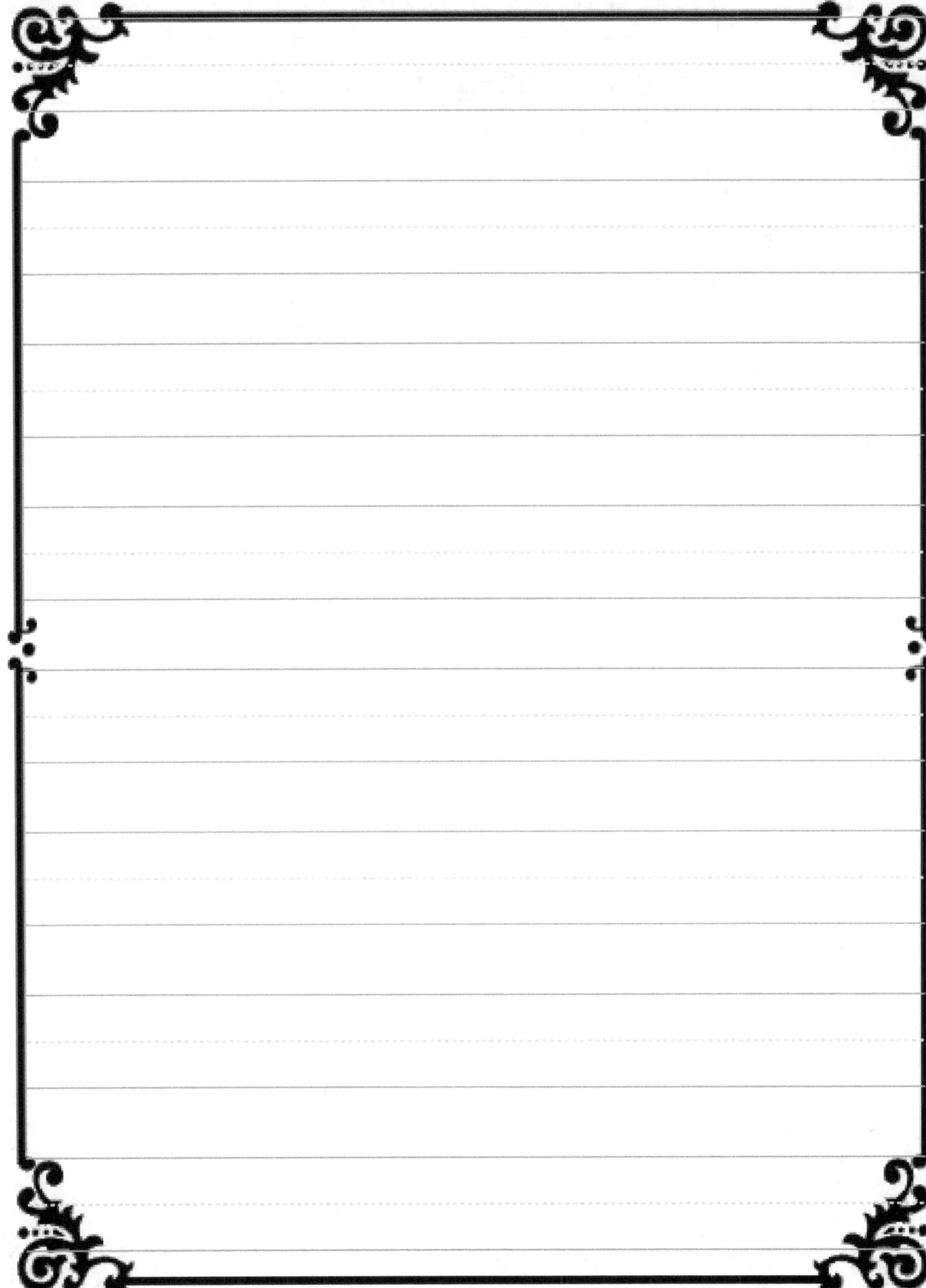

Trace The Letters

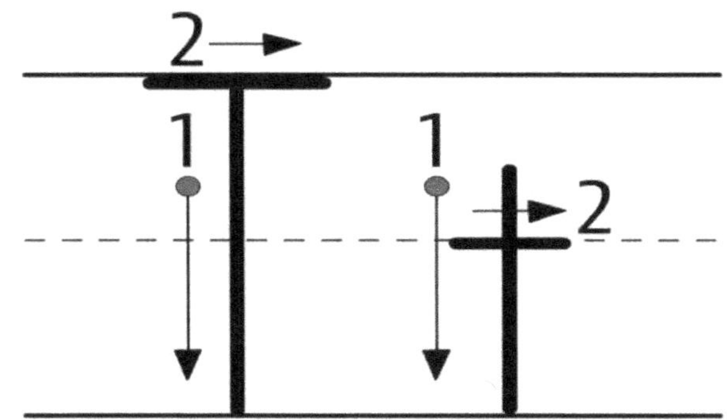

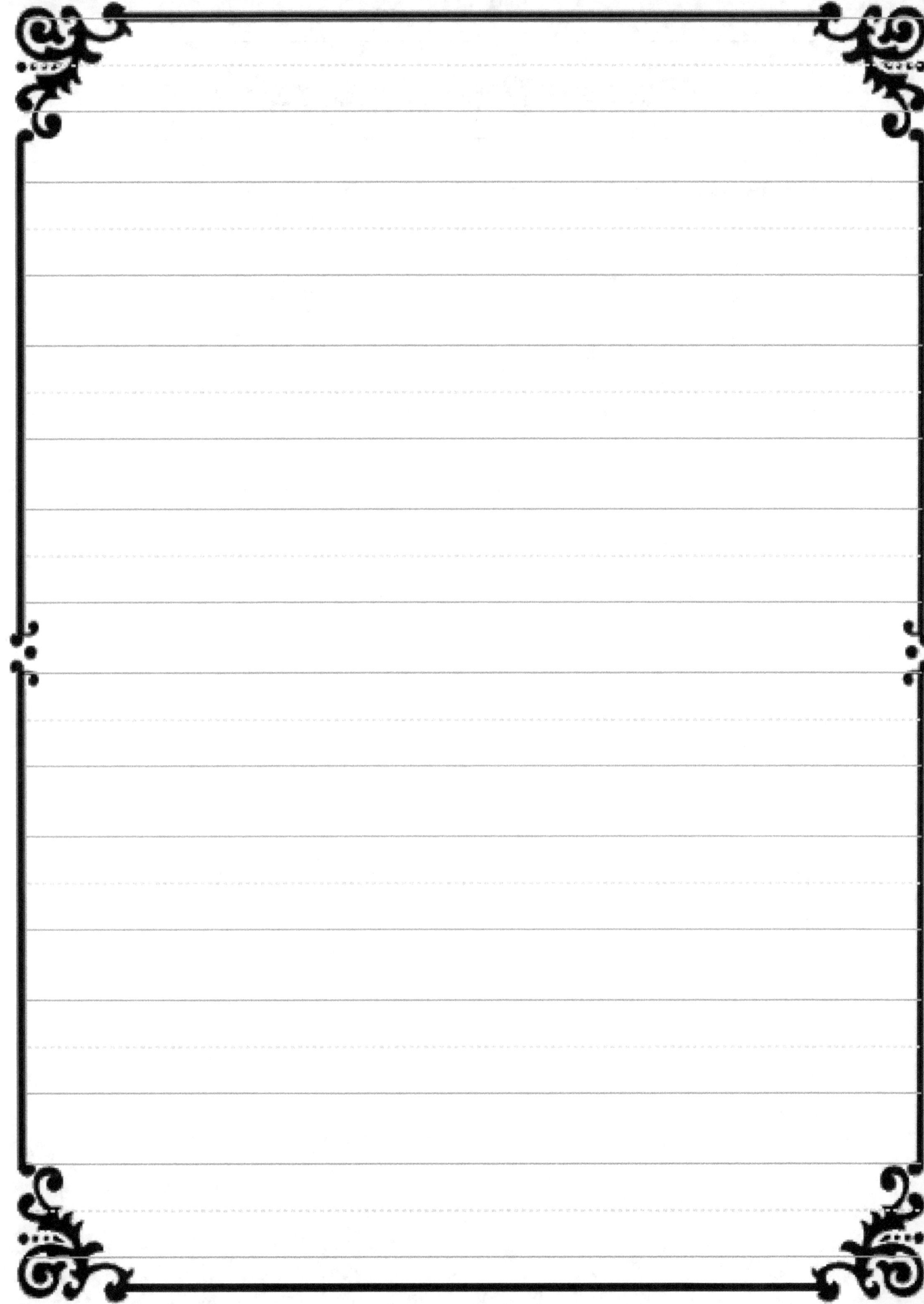

Trace The Letters

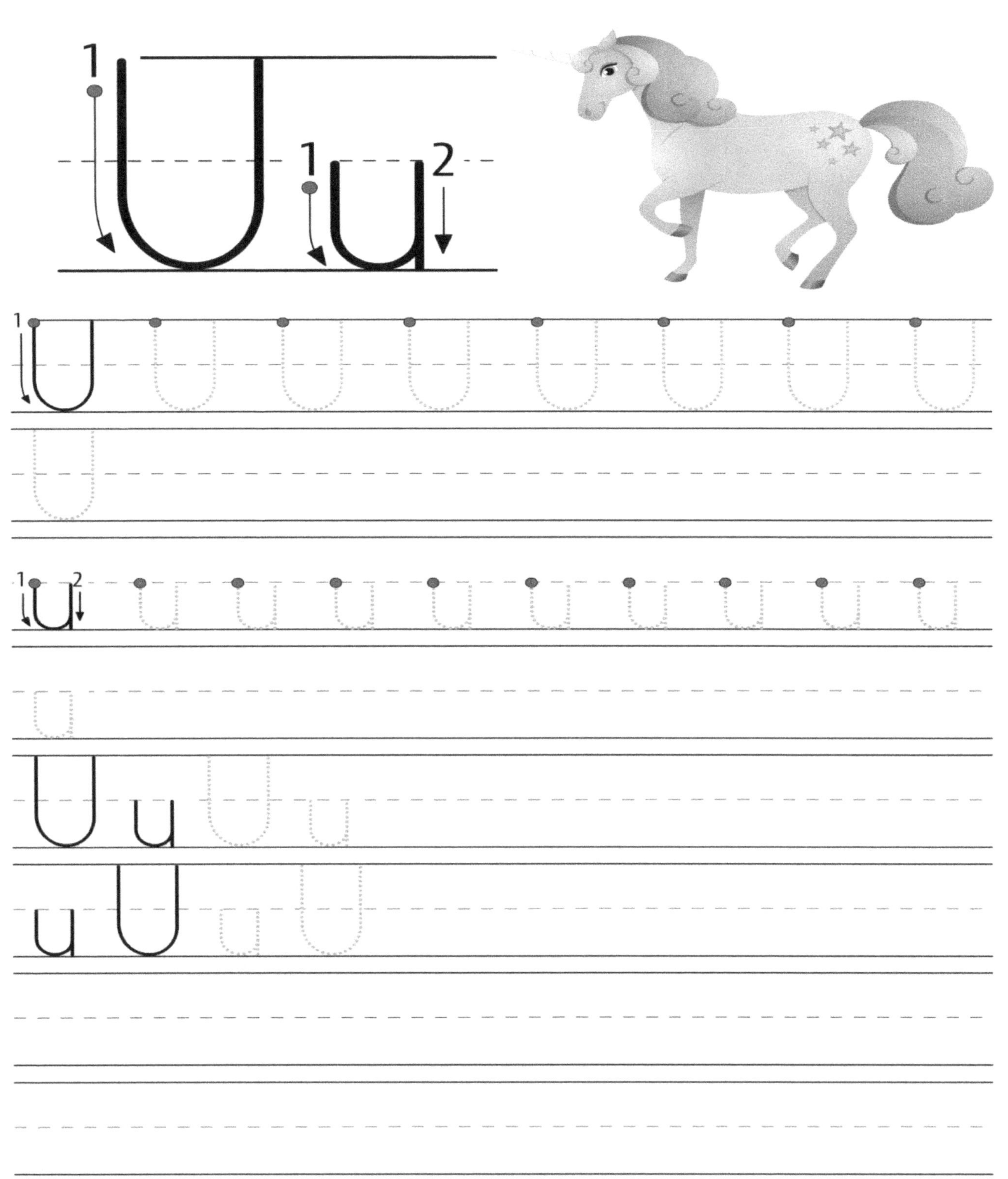

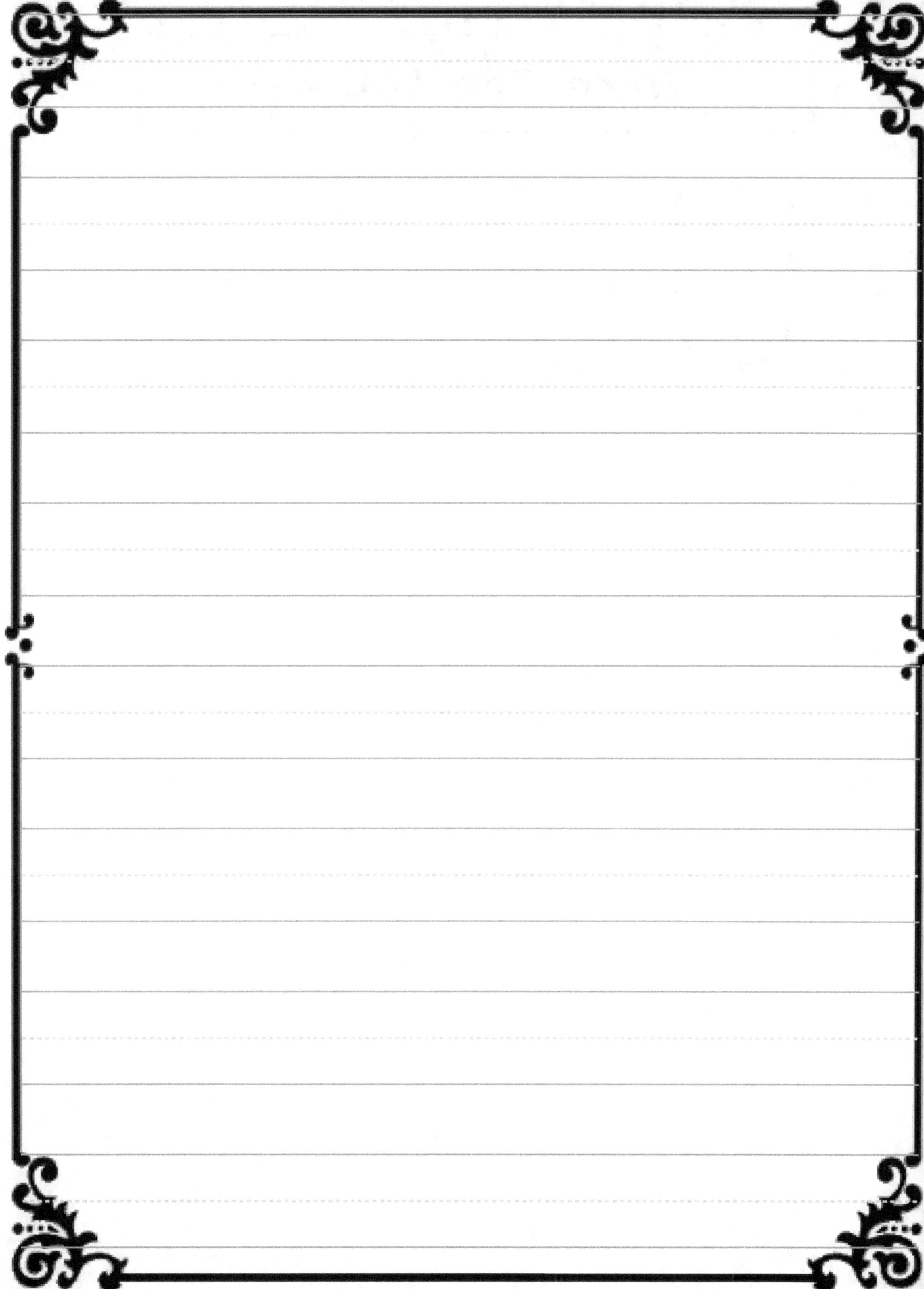

Trace The Letters

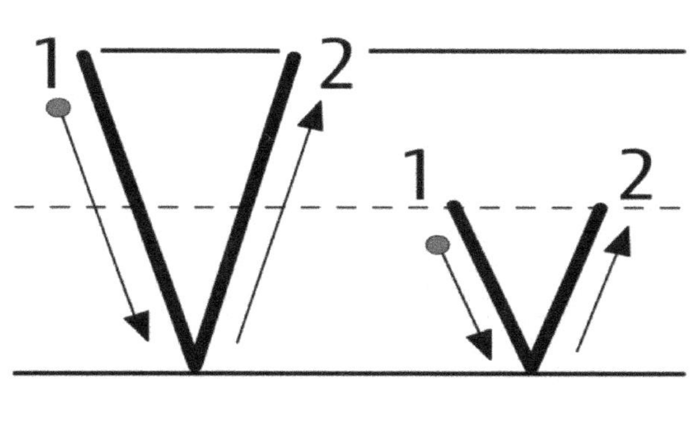

Trace The Letters

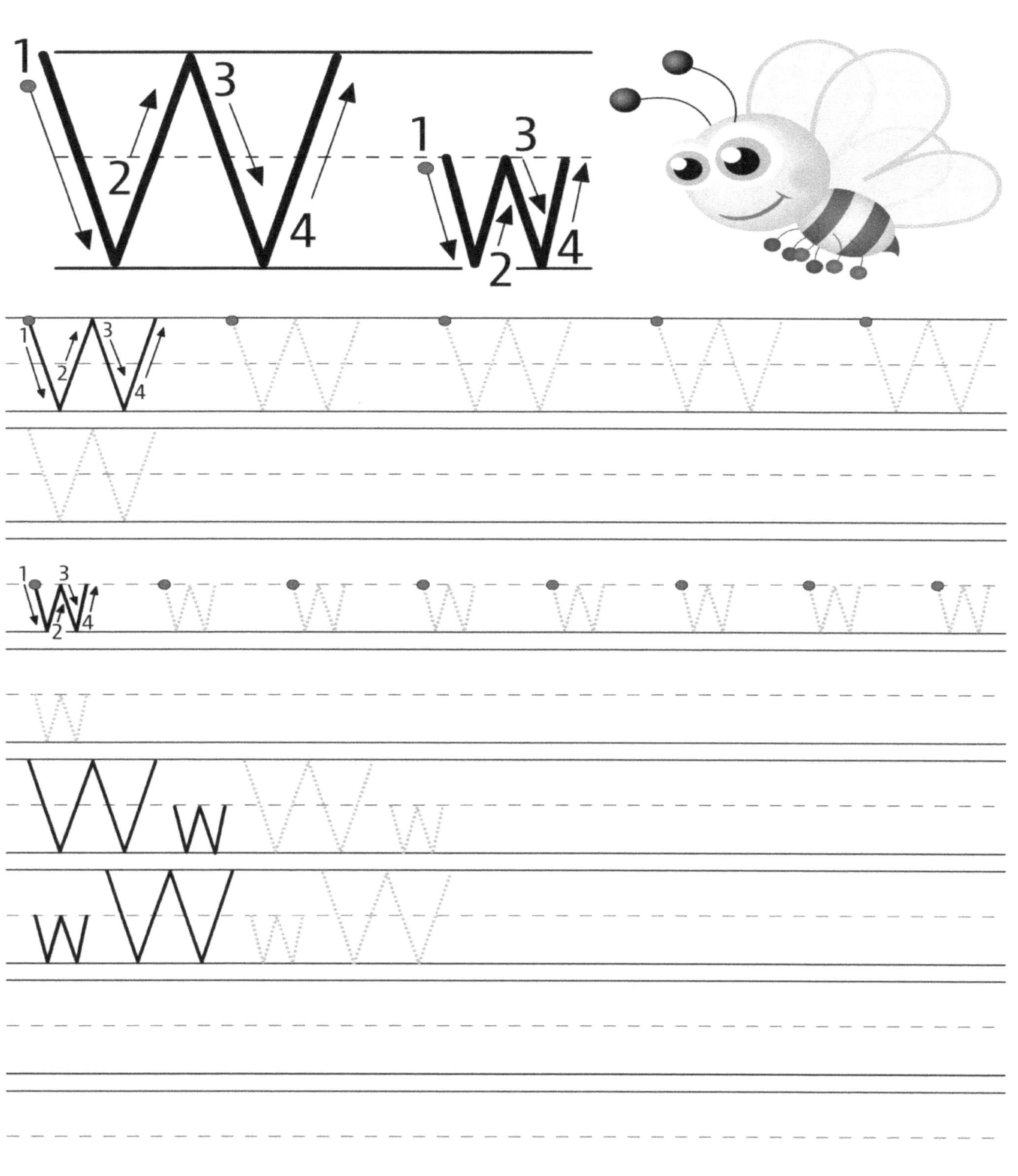

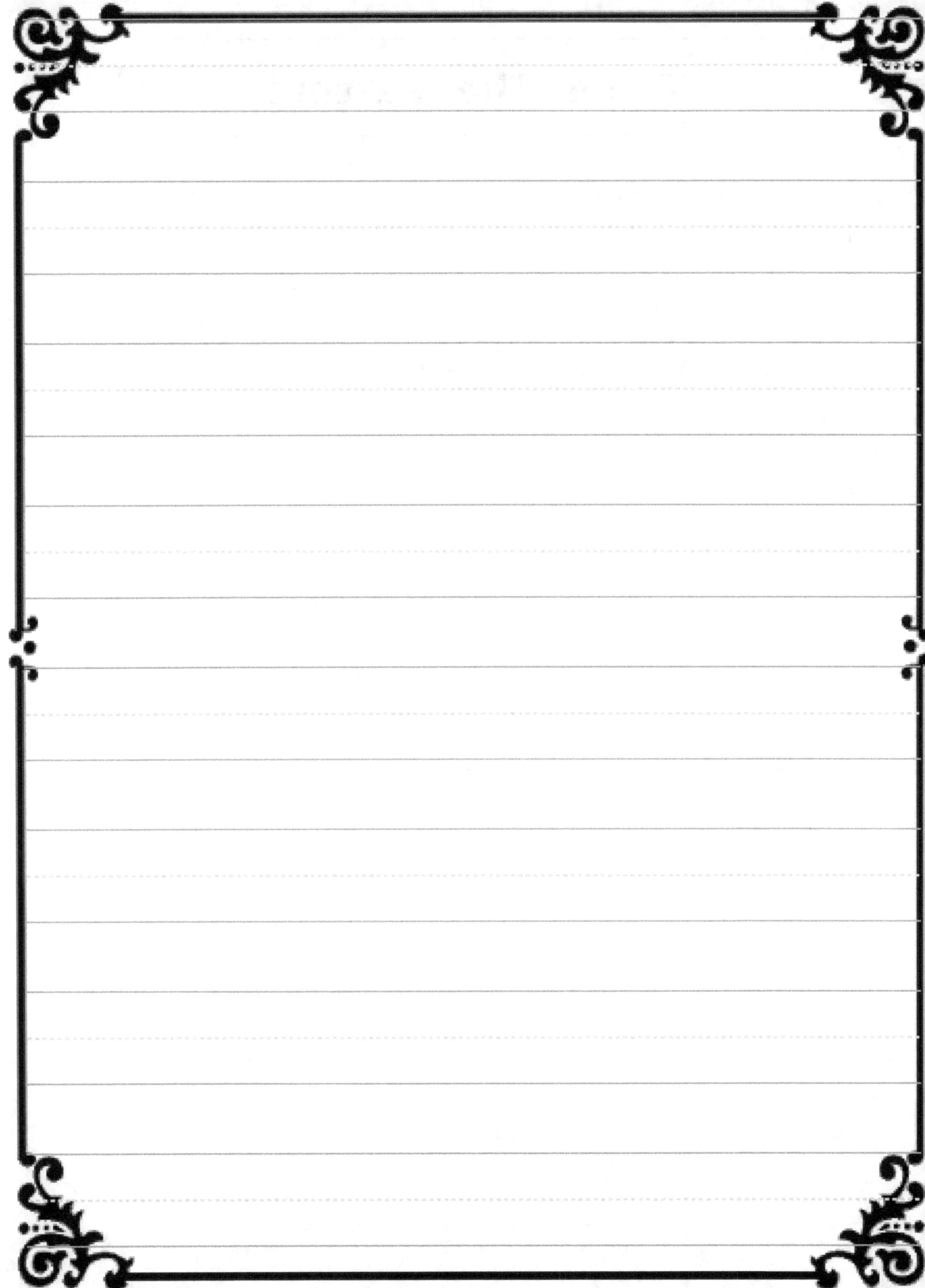

Trace The Letters

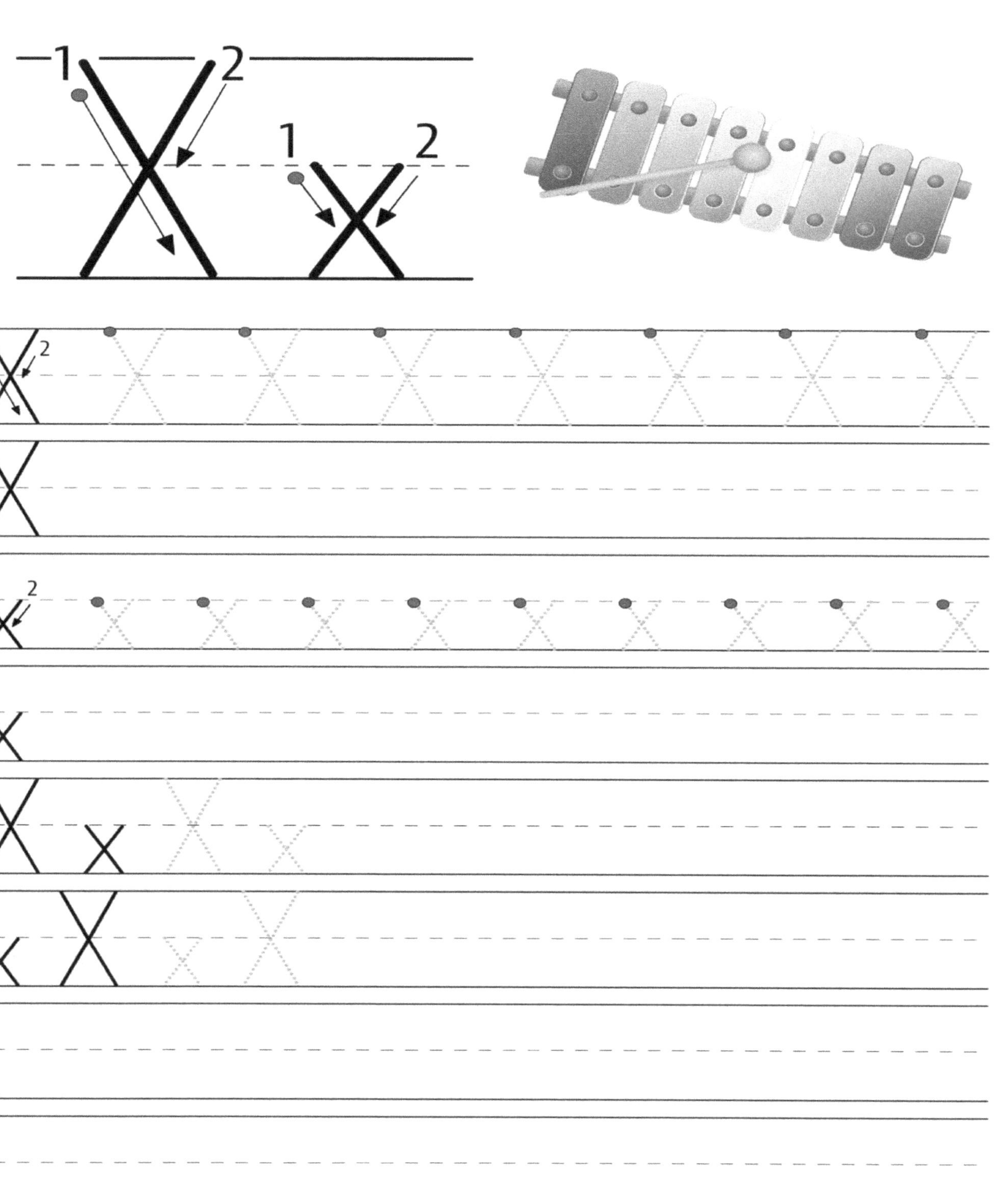

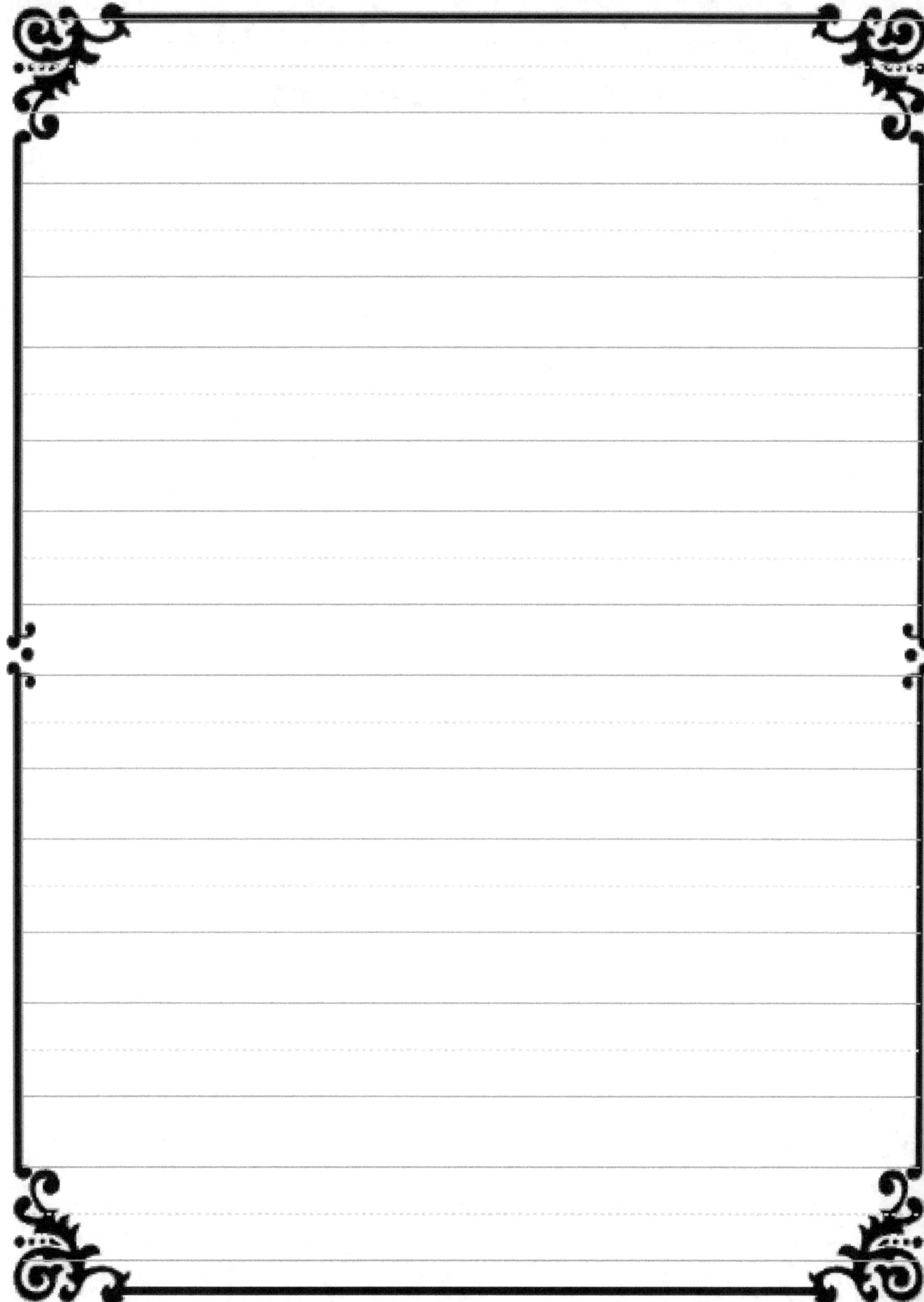

Trace The Letters

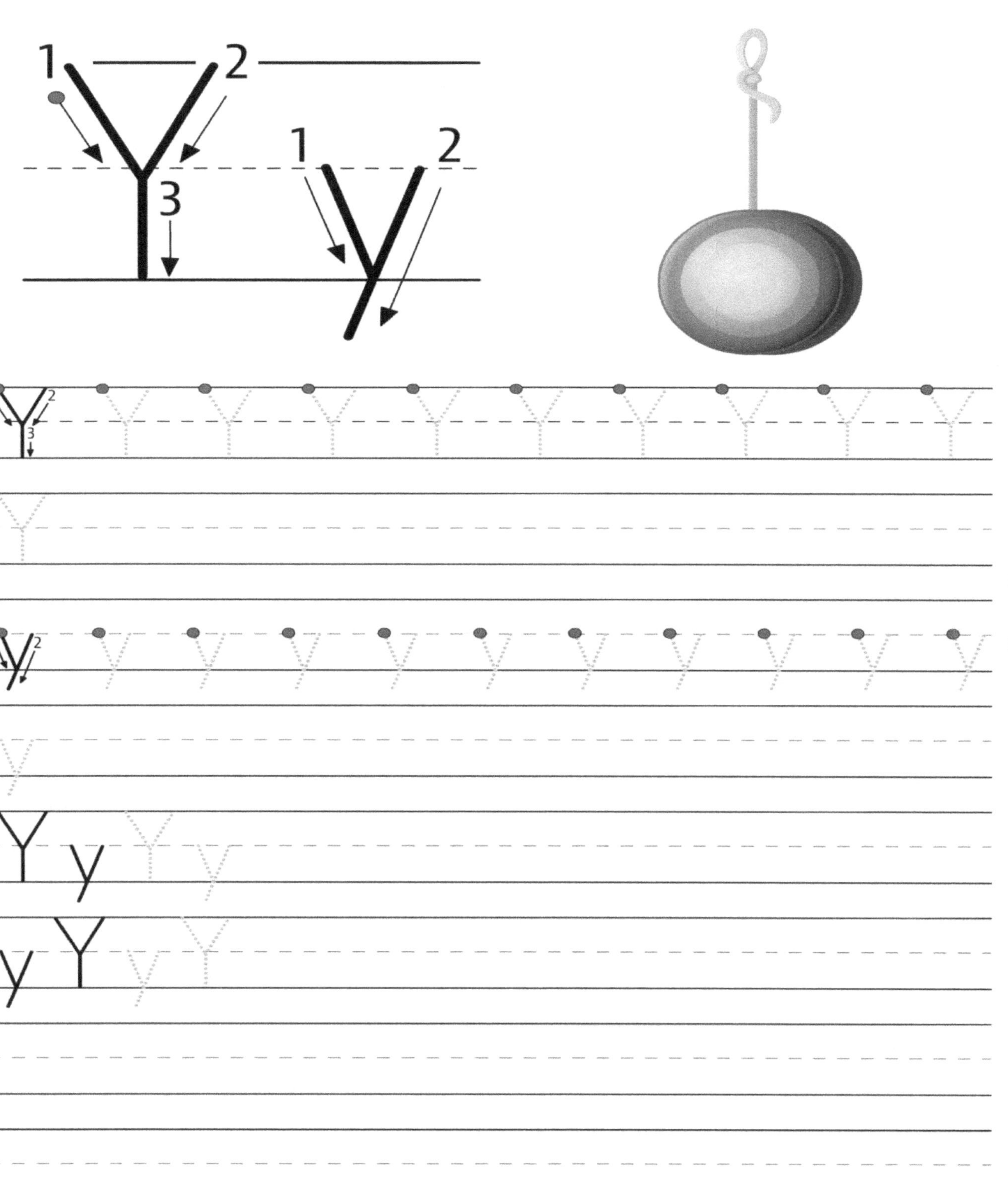

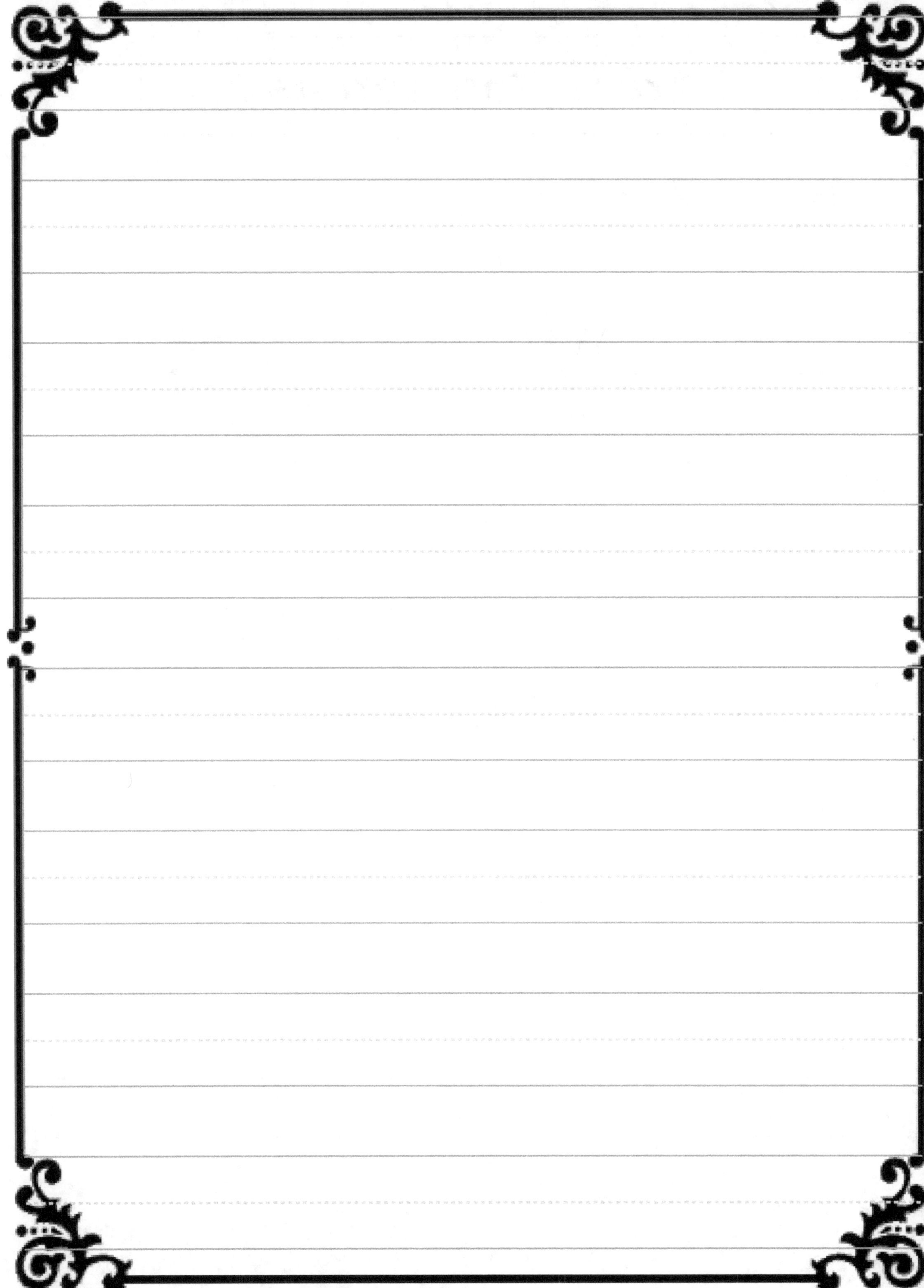

Trace The Letters

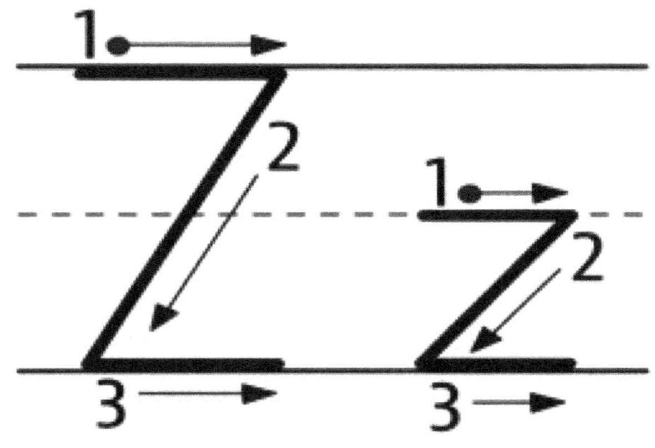

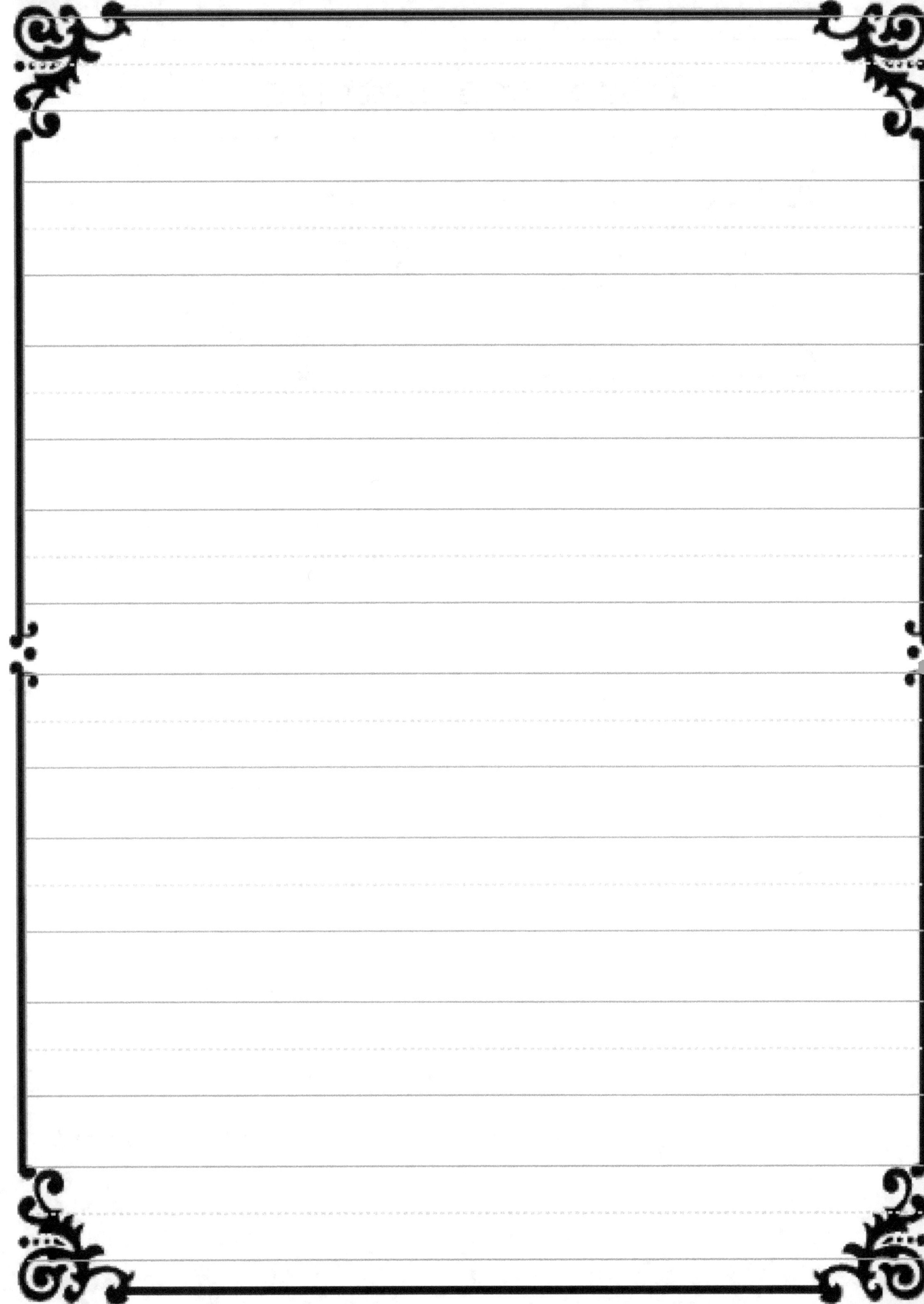